Spring Boot Cookbook

Over 35 recipes to help you build, test, and run Spring applications using Spring Boot

Alex Antonov

BIRMINGHAM - MUMBAI

Spring Boot Cookbook

First published: September 2015

Production reference: 1240915

Published by Packt Publishing Ltd.
Livery Place
35 Livery Street
Birmingham B3 2PB, UK.

ISBN 978-1-78528-415-1

www.packtpub.com

Credits

Author
Alex Antonov

Reviewers
Theo Pack
Eric Pirard
Geoffroy Warin
Ricky Yim

Commissioning Editor
Dipali Goankar

Acquisition Editor
Sonali Vernekar

Content Development Editor
Shweta Pant

Technical Editor
Bharat Patil

Copy Editor
Tasneem Fatehi

Project Coordinator
Shipra Chawhan

Proofreader
Safis Editing

Indexer
Monica Ajmera Mehta

Production Coordinator
Arvindkumar Gupta

Cover Work
Arvindkumar Gupta

About the Author

Alex Antonov is a very passionate technologist with a hunger to learn new tools, languages, techniques, and concepts behind enterprise application design. His specialty lies in designing highly scalable distributed large-scale enterprise systems, which he has been successfully doing for the last 12 years. He is also a frequent presenter on the topics of architecture and design at conferences such as UberConf, JavaOne, and Spring 2GX.

Alex joined Orbitz Worldwide in 2004, and in his current role of Senior Principal Engineer, he is responsible for providing technical leadership and guidance in the development of foundational technologies, core libraries, and APIs for enterprise-wide use, as well as establishing and maintaining common design principles and standards used within the company and integration of new software development practices within the development community. He has extensive experience in enterprise architecture designing distributed systems, and spends a lot of time doing object domain modeling and focusing on domain-driven design and behavior-driven development and testing. Prior to that, Alex was a lead engineer in the same team that was responsible for web application frameworks and developing common practices and additional functionality on top of Spring MVC and Webflow.

He has been a long-time Spring user, starting with Spring 2.0.8 and all the way to the latest and greatest—Spring Boot. Ever since the introduction of Spring Boot, he has been writing applications using the framework as well as contributing patches to the codebase. His general interests lie in the area of distributed computing and technologies and frameworks that enable ease of application creation and cross communication. Besides Java, he is also proficient in Ruby/Rails, PHP, Groovy and is currently learning Erlang.

Alex is a graduate of Loyola University of Chicago, with a BS in computer science and an MS in computer science specializing in software architecture. He currently resides in Evanston, IL. When not coding, Alex enjoys playing tennis, hiking, skiing, and traveling.

Acknowledgment

I would like to thank all the people who have inspired, supported, and encouraged me through the book writing process. For me, this book represents the ability to take my passion to build software, my appreciation of the Spring family of frameworks and the amazing work that was done by their creators, combine it with many years of my first-hand experience building complex applications and share all the thoughts and best practices, which I've developed over time and always wanted to share, with the community, to help them build better, more elegant, robust, and performant applications.

I want to specially thank my wife, Alla, for constantly being there for me, for supporting me in writing this book, for being understanding when I spent countless evenings and weekends working on the chapters, for giving me an extra push to the finish line, when I was close to being done and for just being there for me! Honey, I love you very much!!!

A special thank you goes to my parents, for giving me the opportunity to pursue my carrier dreams, for the education, and raising me to become the person I am. All your hard work is now paying off, and I would not be able to achieve what I had, and write this book, if it weren't for you. I love you guys a lot, and while you are around, I can still be a child.

About the Reviewers

Theo Pack is a software engineer with several years of experience in developing frontend and backend applications. He completed his M.Sc. and has been working at Cologne Intelligence GmbH, a consulting company in Germany, since 2009.

Theo is passionate about technology and likes to master new programming languages.

You can read his blog at `http://furikuri.github.io` or follow him on Twitter at `@furikuri`.

Eric Pirard is a Java developer from the past few years. He is interested in the new technologies that help developers in their jobs to satisfy the customer's requirements as quick as possible. He also likes to help his friends or colleagues in solving their problems and progressing in their projects if he can.

As there are a lot of things to do in addition to his exciting job, if technology can help to solve customers problems as soon as possible, he is very interested. In this way, he has more time to spend with his family, enjoying sports, travelling, in short, enjoying life.

Geoffroy Warin has been programming since he was 10. He is a firm believer in the software craftsmanship movement and open source initiatives. A developer by choice and conviction, he has been working on the conception of enterprise-level web applications in Java and JavaScript throughout the course of his career.

He also teaches courses on Java web stacks and is a Groovy and Spring enthusiast.

You can read more about him on his blog at `http://geowarin.github.io` and on Twitter at `@geowarin`.

Ricky Yim is a passionate software engineer who has over 15 years of industry experience. He is a firm believer in using test-driven and behavior-driven development and agile practices to solve problems. He takes a flexible approach to software delivery and applies innovative solutions. He is currently the Delivery Manager for DiUS, an Australian technology services organization, `http://www.dius.com.au`.

You can find out more about him at http://codingricky.com, and you can follow him on GitHub at http://github.com/codingricky and on Twitter at `@codingricky`. He is also an avid runner and you can read about his adventures here at `http://runningricky.com`.

www.PacktPub.com

Support files, eBooks, discount offers, and more

For support files and downloads related to your book, please visit www.PacktPub.com.

Did you know that Packt offers eBook versions of every book published, with PDF and ePub files available? You can upgrade to the eBook version at www.PacktPub.com and as a print book customer, you are entitled to a discount on the eBook copy. Get in touch with us at service@packtpub.com for more details.

At www.PacktPub.com, you can also read a collection of free technical articles, sign up for a range of free newsletters and receive exclusive discounts and offers on Packt books and eBooks.

https://www2.packtpub.com/books/subscription/packtlib

Do you need instant solutions to your IT questions? PacktLib is Packt's online digital book library. Here, you can search, access, and read Packt's entire library of books.

Why Subscribe?

- ▶ Fully searchable across every book published by Packt
- ▶ Copy and paste, print, and bookmark content
- ▶ On demand and accessible via a web browser

Free Access for Packt account holders

If you have an account with Packt at www.PacktPub.com, you can use this to access PacktLib today and view 9 entirely free books. Simply use your login credentials for immediate access.

Table of Contents

Preface

Spring Boot gives you the ability to create modern enterprise applications using a convention-over-configuration design principle and building on the power and flexibility of the underlying Spring Framework and its various components.

This book will help readers to create different types of Spring Boot applications, understand how to configure their behavior, and write and add custom components. They will obtain knowledge in how to be more efficient in testing, deploying, and monitoring their applications, which will help them through all the stages of the Software Development Life Cycle. By the end of the book, readers will have gained the skills and expertise to deploy and develop applications using Spring Boot.

What this book covers

Chapter 1, Getting Started with Spring Boot, provides you with an overview of the important and useful Spring Boot starters that are included in the framework. You will learn how to use the http://spring.io/ resources, how to get started with a simple project, configure the build file to contain your desired starters, and finish by creating a simple command-line application configured to execute some scheduled tasks.

Chapter 2, Configuring Web Application, provides you with examples of how to create and add the custom ServletFilters, Interceptors, Converters, Formatters and PropertyEditors to a Spring Boot web application. It will start by creating a new web application and proceed to use it as a base to customize with the above mentioned components.

Chapter 3, Web Framework Behavior Tuning, delves into fine-tuning the behavior of a web application. It will cover configuring the custom routing rules and patterns, adding additional static asset paths, and adding and modifying the servlet container connectors and other properties such as enabling SSL.

Chapter 4, Writing Custom Spring Boot Starters, shows you how to create custom Spring Boot Starters in order to provide additional behaviors and functionalities that might be required for complex enterprise applications. You will learn about the inner workings of the autoconfiguration mechanics and how to use them to selectively enable/disable default functionalities and conditionally load your own.

Chapter 5, Application Testing, explores the different techniques to test Spring Boot applications. It starts by introducing you to the testing of MVC applications, then proceeds with some tips on how to use the in-memory database with prepopulated data in order to mimic the real DB interactions during tests, and concludes with examples of behavior-driven development via testing tools such as Cucumber and Spock.

Chapter 6, Application Packaging and Deployment, shows you how every written application needs to be deployed. You will see examples of configuring their build to produce Docker images and self-executing binary files for the Linux/OSX environments. It will explore the options to configure the external applications using Consul and delve into the details of the Spring Boot environment and configuration functionalities.

Chapter 7, Health Monitoring and Data Visualization, explores the various mechanisms that Spring Boot provides to help us see the data about our application's health. It will start by showing you how to write and expose the custom health metrics and see the data using the http endpoints and JMX. It will then proceed with the overview and creation of the management commands for CRaSH and finish with the integration of the monitoring data with Graphite and Dashing using the Codahale/Dropwizard Metrics framework.

What you need for this book

For this book, you need JDK 1.8 installed in your favorite operating system: Linux, Windows, or OS X.

The rest of the software such as the Gradle build tool, all the necessary Java libraries such as Spring Boot and Spring Framework, and their dependencies as well as Docker, Consul, Graphite, Grafana, and Dashing will all be installed through the recipes in this book.

Who this book is for

This book is targeted at the Java developers who have a good knowledge level and an understanding of the Spring and Java application development, are familiar with the notions of Software Development Life Cycle (SDLC), and understand the need for different kinds of testing strategies, general monitoring, and deployment concerns. This book is for those who want to learn efficient Spring Boot development techniques, integration, and extension capabilities in order to make the existing development process more efficient.

Conventions

In this book, you will find a number of styles of text that distinguish between the different kinds of information. Here are some examples of these styles and an explanation of their meaning.

Code words in text, database table names, folder names, filenames, file extensions, pathnames, dummy URLs, user input, and Twitter handles are shown as follows: "We can include other contexts through the use of the `include` directive."

A block of code is set as follows:

```
public class StartupRunner implements CommandLineRunner {
  protected final Log logger = LogFactory.getLog(getClass());
  @Autowired
  private DataSourceds;
  @Override
  public void run(String... args) throws Exception {
    logger.info("DataSource: "+ds.toString());
  }
}
```

Any command-line input or output is written as follows:

spring.datasource.driver-class-name: com.mysql.jdbc.Driver

spring.datasource.url: jdbc:mysql://localhost:3306/springbootcookbook

spring.datasource.username: root

spring.datasource.password:

New terms and **important words** are shown in bold. Words that you see on the screen, in menus or dialog boxes for example, appear in the text like this: " Clicking on **Generate Project** will download a premade project skeleton for us to start with.".

 Warnings or important notes appear in a box like this.

 Tips and tricks appear like this.

Reader feedback

Feedback from our readers is always welcome. Let us know what you think about this book—what you liked or may have disliked. Reader feedback is important for us to develop titles that you really get the most out of.

To send us general feedback, simply send an e-mail to feedback@packtpub.com, and mention the book title via the subject of your message.

If there is a topic that you have expertise in and you are interested in either writing or contributing to a book, see our author guide on www.packtpub.com/authors.

Customer support

Now that you are the proud owner of a Packt book, we have a number of things to help you to get the most from your purchase.

Downloading the example code

You can download the example code files for all Packt books you have purchased from your account at http://www.packtpub.com. If you purchased this book elsewhere, you can visit http://www.packtpub.com/support and register to have the files e-mailed directly to you.

Errata

Although we have taken every care to ensure the accuracy of our content, mistakes do happen. If you find a mistake in one of our books—maybe a mistake in the text or the code—we would be grateful if you would report this to us. By doing so, you can save other readers from frustration and help us improve subsequent versions of this book. If you find any errata, please report them by visiting http://www.packtpub.com/submit-errata, selecting your book, clicking on the **errata submission form** link, and entering the details of your errata. Once your errata are verified, your submission will be accepted and the errata will be uploaded on our website, or added to any list of existing errata, under the Errata section of that title. Any existing errata can be viewed by selecting your title from http://www.packtpub.com/support.

Piracy

Piracy of copyright material on the Internet is an ongoing problem across all media. At Packt, we take the protection of our copyright and licenses very seriously. If you come across any illegal copies of our works, in any form, on the Internet, please provide us with the location address or website name immediately so that we can pursue a remedy.

Please contact us at copyright@packtpub.com with a link to the suspected pirated material.

We appreciate your help in protecting our authors, and our ability to bring you valuable content.

Questions

You can contact us at questions@packtpub.com if you are having a problem with any aspect of the book, and we will do our best to address it.

1

Getting Started with Spring Boot

Spring Boot has a lot of starters that are already a part of the Spring Boot family. This chapter will provide you with an overview of `http://start.spring.io/`, available components provided by Spring Boot, and will also show you how to make a project *Bootiful*, as Josh Long likes to call it.

In this chapter, we will learn about the following topics:

- ▶ Using a Spring Boot template and starter
- ▶ Creating a simple application
- ▶ Launching an application using Gradle
- ▶ Using the command-line runners
- ▶ Setting up a database connection
- ▶ Setting up a data repository service
- ▶ Scheduling executors

Introduction

In a fast-paced world of today's software development, the speed of an application creation and the need for rapid prototyping are becoming more and more important. If you are developing a software using a JVM language, Spring Boot is exactly the kind of framework that will give you the power combined with the flexibility that will enable you to produce high-quality software at a rapid pace. So, let's take a look at how Spring Boot can help you to make your application *Bootiful*.

Using a Spring Boot template and starters

Spring Boot comes with over 40 different starter modules, which provide ready-to-use integration libraries for many different frameworks, such as database connections that are both relational and NoSQL, web services, social network integration, monitoring libraries, logging, template rendering, and the list just keeps going. While it is not practically feasible to cover every single one of these components, we will go over the important and popular ones in order to get an idea of the realm of possibilities and the ease of application development that Spring Boot provides us with.

How to do it...

We will start with creating a basic simple project skeleton and Spring Boot will help us in this:

1. Let's head over to `http://start.spring.io`.
2. Fill out a simple form with the details about our project.
3. Clicking on **Generate Project** will download a premade project skeleton for us to start with.

How it works...

You will see the **Project Dependencies** section, where we can choose the kind of functionalities that our application will perform: will it connect to a database, will it have a web interface, do we plan to integrate with any of the social networks, provide runtime operational support capabilities, and so on. By selecting the desired technologies, the appropriate starter libraries will be added automatically to the dependency list of our pregenerated project template.

Before we proceed with the generation of our project, let's go over exactly what a Spring Boot starter is and the benefits it provides us with.

Spring Boot aims to simplify the process of getting started with an application creation. Spring Boot starters are bootstrap libraries that contain a collection of all the relevant transitive dependencies that are needed to start a particular functionality. Each starter has a special file, which contains the list of all the provided dependencies—`spring.provides`. Let's take a look at the following link for a `spring-boot-starter-test` definition as an example:

`https://github.com/spring-projects/spring-boot/blob/master/spring-boot-starters/spring-boot-starter-test/src/main/resources/META-INF/spring.provides`

Here we will see the following:

```
provides: spring-test, spring-boot, junit, mockito, hamcrest-library
```

This tells us that by including `spring-boot-starter-test` in our build as a dependency, we will automatically get `spring-test`, `spring-boot`, `junit`, `mockito`, and `hamcrest-library`. These libraries will provide us with all the necessary things in order to start writing application tests for the software that we will develop, without needing to manually add these dependencies to the build file individually.

With more than 40 starters provided and with the ongoing community additions increasing the list, it is very likely that in case we find ourselves with the need to integrate with a fairly common or popular framework, there is already a starter out there that we can use.

The following table shows you the most notable ones so as to give you an idea of what is available:

Starter	Description
`spring-boot-starter`	This is the core Spring Boot starter that provides you with all the foundational functionalities. It is depended upon by all other starters, so there is no need to declare it explicitly.
`spring-boot-starter-actuator`	This starter provides you with a functionality to monitor, manage an application, and audit it.
`spring-boot-starter-jdbc`	This starter provides you with a support to connect and use JDBC databases, connection pools, and so on.
`spring-boot-starter-data-jpa`	The JPA starter provides you with needed libraries in order to use Java Persistence API such as Hibernate, and others.
`spring-boot-starter-data-*`	Collection of `data-*` family starter components providing support for a number of data stores such as MongoDB, Data-Rest, or Solr.
`spring-boot-starter-security`	This brings in all the needed dependencies for `spring-security`.
`spring-boot-starter-social-*`	This provides you with integration with Facebook, Twitter, and LinkedIn.
`spring-boot-starter-test`	This is a starter that contains the dependencies for `spring-test` and assorted testing frameworks such as JUnit and Mockito among others.
`spring-boot-starter-web`	This gives you all the needed dependencies for web application development. It can be complimented with `spring-boot-starter-hateoas`, `spring-boot-starter-websocket`, `spring-boot-starter-mobile`, or `spring-boot-starter-ws`, and assorted template rendering starters such as `sping-boot-starter-thymeleaf` or `spring-boot-starter-mustache`.

Creating a simple application

Now that we have a basic idea of the starters that are available to us, let's go ahead and create our application template at `http://start.spring.io`.

How to do it...

The application that we are going to create is a book catalog management system. It will keep a record of books that were published, who were the authors, the reviewers, publishing houses, and so forth. We will name our project `BookPub`, and apply the following steps:

1. Use the default proposed **Group** name: `org.test`.

2. Enter `bookpub` for an **Artifact** field.

3. Provide `BookPub` as a **Name** for the application.

4. Specify `org.test.bookpub` as our **Package Name**.

5. Choose **Gradle Project**.

6. Select `Jar` as **Packaging**.

7. Use **Java Version** as `1.8`.

8. Use **Spring Boot Version** as `1.2.5`.

9. Select the **H2**, **JDBC**, and **JPA** starters from the **Project Dependencies** selection so that we can get the needed artifacts in our build file in order to connect to an H2 database

10. Click **Generate Project** to download the project archive.

How it works...

Clicking on the **Generate Project** button will download the `bookpub.zip` archive, which we will extract in our working directory. In the newly created `bookpub` directory, we will see a `build.gradle` file that defines our build. It already comes preconfigured with the right version of a Spring Boot plugin and libraries and even includes the extra starters, which we have chosen.

The following is the code of the `build.gradle` file:

```
dependencies {
  compile("org.springframework.boot:spring-boot-starter-data-jpa")
  compile("org.springframework.boot:spring-boot-starter-jdbc")
  runtime("com.h2database:h2")
  testCompile("org.springframework.boot:spring-boot-starter-test")
}
```

We have selected the following starters:

- ► `org.springframework.boot:spring-boot-starter-data-jpa` pulls in the JPA dependency

- ► `org.springframework.boot:spring-boot-starter-jdbc` pulls in the JDBC supporting libraries

- ► `com.h2database:h2` is a particular type of database implementation, namely H2

As you can see, the `runtime("com.h2database:h2")` dependency is a runtime one. This is because we don't really need, and probably don't even want, to know the exact kind of a database to which we will connect at the compile time. Spring Boot will autoconfigure the needed settings and create appropriate beans once it detects the presence of the `org.h2.Driver` class in the classpath when the application is launched. We will look into the inner workings of how and where this happens later in this chapter.

The `data-jpa` and `jdbc` are Spring Boot starter artifacts. If we look inside these dependency jars once they are downloaded locally by Gradle, or using Maven Central online file repository, we will find that they don't contain any actual classes, only the various metadata. The two containing files that are of particular interest to us are `pom.xml` and `spring.provides`. Let's first look at the `spring.provides` file in the `spring-boot-starter-jdbc.jar` artifact, with the following content:

```
provides: spring-jdbc,spring-tx,tomcat-jdbc
```

This tells us that by having this starter as our dependency, we will transitively get the `spring-jdbc`, `spring-tx`, and `tomcat-jdbc` dependency libraries in our build. The `pom.xml` file contains the proper dependency declarations that will be used by Gradle or Maven to resolve the needed dependencies during the build time. This also applies to our second starter: `spring-boot-starter-data-jpa`. This starter will transitively provide us with the `spring-orm`, `hibernate-entity-manager`, and `spring-data-jpa` libraries.

At this point, we have enough libraries/classes in our application classpath so as to give Spring Boot an idea of what kind of application we are trying to run and what are the kind of facilities and frameworks that need to be configured automatically by Spring Boot in order to stitch things together.

Earlier, we mentioned that the presence of the `org.h2.Driver` class in the classpath will trigger Spring Boot to automatically configure the H2 database connection for our application. To see exactly how this will happen, let's start by looking at our newly created application template, specifically at `BookPubApplication.java` located in the `src/main/java/org/test/bookpub` directory in the root of the project, as follows:

```
package org.test.bookpub;

import org.springframework.boot.SpringApplication;
```

```
import org.springframework.boot.autoconfigure.SpringBootApplication;

@SpringBootApplication
public class BookPubApplication {

  public static void main(String[] args) {
    SpringApplication.run(BookPubApplication.class, args);
  }
}
```

This is effectively our entire and fully runnable application. There's not a whole lot of code here and definitely no mention about configuration or databases anywhere. The key to making magic is the `@SpringBootApplication` meta-annotation. In order to understand what actually happens, we can take a look inside the code definition for this annotation, where we will find the real annotations that will direct Spring Boot to set things up automatically:

```
@Configuration
@EnableAutoConfiguration
@ComponentScan
public @interface SpringBootApplication {…}
```

Let's go through the following list of annotations:

▸ `@Configuration` tells Spring (and not just Spring Boot, as it is a Spring Framework core annotation) that the annotated class contains Spring configuration definitions such as the `@Bean`, `@Component`, and `@Service` declarations, and others.

▸ `@ComponentScan` tells Spring that we want to scan our application packages— starting from the package of our annotated class as a default package root—for the other classes that might be annotated with `@Configuration`, `@Controller`, and other applicable annotations, which Spring will automatically include as part of the context configuration.

▸ `@EnableAutoConfiguration` is a part of the Spring Boot annotation, which is a meta-annotation on its own (you will find that Spring libraries rely very heavily on the meta-annotations in order to group and compose configurations together). It imports the `EnableAutoConfigurationImportSelector` and `AutoConfigurationPackages.Registrar` classes that effectively instruct Spring to automatically configure the conditional beans depending on the classes available in the classpath. (We will cover the inner workings of autoconfiguration in detail in *Chapter 4, Writing Custom Spring Boot Starters*).

The `SpringApplication.run(BookPubApplication.class, args);` line in the main method basically creates a Spring application context that reads the annotations in `BookPubApplication.class` and instantiates a context, which is similar to how it would have been done if instead of using Spring Boot we would have stuck with the regular Spring Framework.

Launching an application using Gradle

Typically, the very first step of creating any application is to have a basic skeleton, which can be immediately launched as is. As the Spring Boot starter has created the application template for us already, all we have to do is extract the code, build, and execute it. Now let's go to the console and launch the app with Gradle.

How to do it...

1. Change in the directory where the `bookpub.zip` archive was extracted from and execute the following command from the command line:

   ```
   $ ./gradlew clean bootRun
   ```

 If you don't have `gradlew` in the directory, then download a version of Gradle from `https://gradle.org/downloads` or install it via homebrew by executing `brew install gradle`. After Gradle is installed, run `gradle wrapper` to get the Gradle wrapper files generated. Another way is to invoke `gradle clean bootRun` in order to achieve the same results.

The output of the preceding command will be as follows:

```
...

  .   ____          _            __ _ _
 /\\ / ___'_ __ _ _(_)_ __  __ _ \ \ \ \
( ( )\___ | '_ | '_| | '_ \/ _` | \ \ \ \
 \\/  ___)| |_)| | | | | || (_| |  ) ) ) )
  '  |____| .__|_| |_|_| |_\__, | / / / /
 =========|_|==============|___/=/_/_/_/
 :: Spring Boot ::   (v1.2.3.BUILD-SNAPSHOT)


2015-03-09 23:18:53.721 : Starting BookPubApplication on mbp with PID
43850
2015-03-09 23:18:53.781 : Refreshing org.springframework.context.
annotation.Annotatio
2015-03-09 23:18:55.544 : Building JPA container EntityManagerFactory for
persistence
2015-03-09 23:18:55.565 : HHH000204: Processing PersistenceUnitInfo
[name: default
2015-03-09 23:18:55.624 : Hibernate Core {4.3.8.Final}
2015-03-09 23:18:55.625 : HHH000206: hibernate.properties not found
```

```
2015-03-09 23:18:55.627 : HHH000021: Bytecode provider name : javassist

2015-03-09 23:18:55.774 : HCANN000001: Hibernate Commons Annotations
{4.0.5.Final

2015-03-09 23:18:55.850 : HHH000400: Using dialect: org.hibernate.
dialect.H2Dialect

2015-03-09 23:18:55.902 : HHH000397: Using ASTQueryTranslatorFactory

2015-03-09 23:18:56.094 : HHH000227: Running hbm2ddl schema export

2015-03-09 23:18:56.096 : HHH000230: Schema export complete

2015-03-09 23:18:56.337 : Registering beans for JMX exposure on startup

2015-03-09 23:18:56.345 : Started BookPubApplication in 3.024 seconds
(JVM running...

2015-03-09 23:18:56.346 : Closing org.springframework.context.annotation.
AnnotationC..

2015-03-09 23:18:56.347 : Unregistering JMX-exposed beans on shutdown

2015-03-09 23:18:56.349 : Closing JPA EntityManagerFactory for
persistence unit 'def...

2015-03-09 23:18:56.349 : HHH000227: Running hbm2ddl schema export

2015-03-09 23:18:56.350 : HHH000230: Schema export complete

BUILD SUCCESSFUL

Total time: 52.323 secs
```

How it works...

As we can see, the application started just fine, but as we didn't add any functionality or configure any services, it terminated right away. From the startup log, however, we do see that the autoconfiguration did take place. Let's take a look at the following lines:

```
Building JPA container EntityManagerFactory for persistence unit
'default'
HHH000412: Hibernate Core {4.3.8.Final}
HHH000400: Using dialect: org.hibernate.dialect.H2Dialect
```

This information tells us that because we added the jdbc and data-jpa starters, the JPA container was created and will use Hibernate 4.3.8.Final to manage the persistence using H2Dialect. This was possible because we had the right classes in the classpath.

Downloading the example code

You can download the example code files for all Packt books you have purchased from your account at http://www.packtpub.com. If you purchased this book elsewhere, you can visit http://www.packtpub.com/support and register to have the files e-mailed directly to you.

Using the command-line runners

With our basic application skeleton ready, let's add some meat to the bones by making our application do something.

Let's start by first creating a class named `StartupRunner`. This will implement the `CommandLineRunner` interface, which basically provides just one method—`public void run(String... args)`—that will get called by Spring Boot only once after the application has started.

How to do it...

1. Create the file named `StartupRunner.java` under the `src/main/java/org/test/bookpub/` directory from the root of our project with the following content:

```
package org.test.bookpub;
import org.apache.commons.logging.Log;
import org.apache.commons.logging.LogFactory;
import org.springframework.boot.CommandLineRunner;
public class StartupRunner implements CommandLineRunner {
  protected final Log logger = LogFactory.getLog(getClass());
  @Override
  public void run(String... args) throws Exception {
    logger.info("Hello");
  }
}
```

2. After we have defined the class, let's proceed by defining it as `@Bean` in the `BookPubApplication.java` application configuration, which is located in the same folder as our newly created `StartupRunner.java`, shown as follows:

```
@Bean
public StartupRunner schedulerRunner() {
  return new StartupRunner();
}
```

How it works...

If we run our application again by executing `$ ./gradlew clean bootRun`, we will get an output that is similar to our previous application startup. However, we will see our `Hello` message in the logs as well, which will look as follows:

**2015-03-10 21:57:51.048 INFO --- org.test.bookpub.StartupRunner
: Hello**

Even though the program will get terminated on execution, at least we made it do something!

Command line runners are a useful functionality to execute the various types of code that only have to be run once, right after application startup. Some may also use this as a place to start various executor threads but Spring Boot provides a better solution for this task, which will be discussed at the end of this chapter. The `CommandLineRunner` interface is used by Spring Boot to scan all of its implementations and invoke each instance's run method with the startup arguments. We can also use an `@Order` annotation or implement an `Ordered` interface so as to define the exact order in which we want Spring Boot to execute them. For example, Spring Batch relies on the runners in order to trigger the execution of the jobs.

As command-line runners are instantiated and executed after the application has started, we can use the dependency injection to our advantage in order to wire in whatever dependencies that we need, such as data sources, services, and other components. These can be utilized later while implementing `run(String... args)` method..

It is important to note that if any exceptions are thrown inside the `run(String... args)` method, this will cause the context to close and an application to shut down. Wrapping the risky code blocks with `try/ catch` is recommended in order to prevent this from happening.

Setting up a database connection

In every application, there is a need to access some data and conduct some operations on it. Most frequently, this source of data is a data store of some kind, namely a database. Spring Boot makes it very easy to get started in order to connect to the database and start consuming the data via the Java Persistence API among others.

Getting ready

In our previous example, we created the basic application that will execute a command-line runner by printing a message in the logs. Let's enhance this application by adding a connection to a database.

Earlier, we already added the necessary `jdbc` and `data-jpa` starters as well as an H2 database dependency to our build file. Now, we will configure an in-memory instance of the H2 database.

In the case of an embedded database such as H2, HSQL, or Derby, no actual configuration is required besides including the dependency on one of these in the build file. When one of these databases is detected in the classpath and a `DataSource` bean dependency is declared in the code, Spring Boot will automatically create one for you.

To demonstrate the fact that just by including the H2 dependency in the classpath, we will automatically get a default database, let's modify our `StartupRunner.java` to look as follows:

```java
public class StartupRunner implements CommandLineRunner {
  protected final Log logger = LogFactory.getLog(getClass());
  @Autowired
  private DataSourceds;
  @Override
  public void run(String... args) throws Exception {
    logger.info("DataSource: "+ds.toString());
  }
}
```

Now, if we proceed with the running of our application, we will see the name of the DataSource printed in the log, as follows:

2015-03-11 21:46:22.067 org.test.bookpub.StartupRunner :DataSource: org. apache.tomcat.jdbc.pool.DataSource@4…{…driverClassName=org.h2.Driver; … }

So, under the hood, Spring Boot recognized that we've autowired a DataSource dependency and automatically created one initializing the in-memory H2 datastore. It is all good and well, but probably not all too useful beyond an early prototyping phase or for the purpose of testing. Who would want a database that goes away with all the data as soon as your application shuts down and you have to start with a clean slate every time you restart the app?

How to do it...

Let's change the defaults in order to create an embedded H2 database that will not store data in-memory, but rather use a file to persist the data in between application restarts.

1. Open the file named `application.properties` under the `src/main/resources` directory from the root of our project and add the following content:

   ```
   spring.datasource.url = jdbc:h2:~/test;DB_CLOSE_DELAY=-1;DB_CLOSE_
   ON_EXIT=FALSE
   spring.datasource.username = sa
   spring.datasource.password =
   ```

2. Start the application by executing `./gradlew clean bootRun` from the command line.

3. Check your home directory and you should see the following file in there: `test.mv.db`.

The user home directory is located under /home/<username> on Linux and under /Users/<username> on OS X.

How it works...

Even though, by default, Spring Boot makes certain assumptions about the database configuration by examining the classpath for the presence of supported database drivers, it provides you with easy configuration options in order to tweak the database access via a set of exposed properties grouped under spring.datasource.

The things that we can configure are the url, username, password, driver-class-name, and so on. If you want to consume the datasource from a JNDI location, where an actual instance of a DataSource is being created outside the application, for example by a container, like JBoss or Tomcat, and shared via JNDI, you can configure this using the spring.datasource.jndi-name property. The complete set of possible properties is fairly large, so we will not go into all of them. However, we will cover more options in *Chapter 5, Application Testing*, where we will talk about mocking data for application tests using a database.

 By looking at various blogs and examples, you might notice that some places use dashes in property names such as driver-class-name while others use camel-cased variants such as driverClassName. In Spring Boot, these are actually two equally supported ways of naming the same property and they get translated into the same thing internally.

If you want to connect to a regular (non-embedded) database, besides just having the appropriate driver library in the classpath, we need to specify the driver of our choice in the configuration. The following snippet is what the configuration to connect to MySQL would resemble:

```
spring.datasource.driver-class-name: com.mysql.jdbc.Driver

spring.datasource.url: jdbc:mysql://localhost:3306/springbootcookbook

spring.datasource.username: root

spring.datasource.password:
```

If we wanted Hibernate to create the schema automatically, based on our entity classes, we will need to add the following line to the configuration:

```
spring.jpa.hibernate.ddl-auto=create-drop
```

 Don't do this in the production environment, otherwise on startup, all the table schemas and data **will be deleted!** Use the update or validate values instead, where needed.

One can go even further in the abstraction layer and instead of auto-wiring a DataSource object, you could go straight for a `JdbcTemplate`. This would instruct Spring Boot to automatically create a DataSource and then create a `JdbcTemplate` wrapping the DataSource, thus providing you with a more convenient way of interacting with a database in a safe way. The code for `JdbcTemplate` is as follows:

```
@Autowired
private JdbcTemplate jdbcTemplate;
```

For the extra curious minds, one can look in the `spring-boot-autoconfigure` source at an `org.springframework.boot.autoconfigure.jdbc.DataSourceAutoConfiguration` class so as to see the code behind the DataSource creation magic.

Setting up a data repository service

Connecting to a database and then executing good old SQL—while simplistic and straightforward—is not the most convenient way to operate on the data, map it in a set of domain objects, and manipulate the relational content. This is why multiple frameworks emerged in order to aid you with mapping the data from tables into objects, better known as Object Relational Mapping. The most notable example of such a framework is Hibernate.

In the previous example, we covered how to set up a connection to a database and configure the settings for the username, password, which driver to use, and so on. In this recipe, we will enhance our application by adding a few entity objects that define the structure of the data in the database and a `CrudRepository` interface to access the data.

As our application is a book tracking catalogue, the obvious domain objects would be the `Book`, `Author`, `Reviewers`, and `Publisher`.

How to do it...

1. Create a new package folder named `entity` under the `src/main/java/org/test/bookpub` directory from the root of our project.

2. In this newly created package, create a new class named `Book` with the following content:

```
@Entity
public class Book {
    @Id
    @GeneratedValue
    private Long id;
    private String isbn;
    private String title;
```

```
    private String description;

    @ManyToOne
    private Author author;
    @ManyToOne
    private Publisher publisher;

    @ManyToMany
    private List<Reviewers> reviewers;

    protected Book() {}

    public Book(String isbn, String title, Author author,
                Publisher publisher) {
      this.isbn= isbn;
      this.title = title;
      this.author= author;
      this.publisher= publisher;
    }
    //Skipping getters and setters to save space, but we do need
  them
  }
```

3. As any book should have an author and a publisher, and ideally some reviewers, we need to create these entity objects as well. Let's start by creating an `Author` entity class under the same directory as our `Book` on, as follows:

```
@Entity
public class Author {
  @Id
  @GeneratedValue
  private Long id;
  private String firstName;
  private String lastName;
  @OneToMany(mappedBy = "author")
  private List<Book> books;

  protected Author() {}

  public Author(String firstName, String lastName) {...}
    //Skipping implementation to save space, but we do need
      it all
}
```

4. Similarly, we will create the `Publisher` and `Reviewer` classes, as shown in the following code:

```
@Entity
public class Publisher {
  @Id
  @GeneratedValue
  private Long id;
  private String name;
  @OneToMany(mappedBy = "publisher")
  private List<Book> books;

  protected Publisher() {}

  public Publisher(String name) {...}
}

@Entity
public class Reviewer {
  @Id
  @GeneratedValue
  private Long id;
  private String firstName;
  private String lastName;

  protected Reviewer() {}

  public Reviewer(String firstName, String lastName) {
    //Skipping implementation to save space
  }
}
```

5. Now, we will create our `BookRepository` interface by extending Spring's `CrudRepository` under the `src/main/java/org/test/bookpub/repository` package, as follows:

```
@Repository
public interface BookRepository extends CrudRepository<Book, Long> {
  public Book findBookByIsbn(String isbn);
}
```

6. Finally, let's modify our `StartupRunner` in order to print the number of books in our collection instead of some random DataSource string by auto-wiring a newly created `BookRepository` and printing the result of a `.count()` call to the log, as follows:

```
public class StartupRunner implements CommandLineRunner {
  @Autowired
  private BookRepository bookRepository;

  public void run(String... args) throws Exception {
    logger.info("Number of books: " +
      bookRepository.count());
  }
}
```

How it works...

As you have probably noticed, we didn't write a single line of SQL or even mentioned anything about database connections, building queries, or things like that. The only hint that we are dealing with the database-backed data that we have in our code are the class and field annotations: `@Entity`, `@Repository`, `@Id`, `@GeneratedValue`, and `@ManyToOne` along with `@ManyToMany` and `@OneToMany`. These annotations, which are a part of the Java Persistence API, along with the extension of the `CrudRepository` interface are our ways of communicating with Spring about the need to map our objects to the appropriate tables and fields in the database and provide us with the programmatic ability to interact with this data.

Let's go through the following annotations:

▶ `@Entity` indicates that the annotated class should be mapped to a database table. The name of the table will be derived from the name of the class but it can be configured, if needed. It is important to note that every entity class should have a default `protected` constructor, which is needed for automated instantiation and Hibernate interactions.

▶ `@Repository` indicates that the interface is intended to provide you with the access and manipulation of data for a database. It also serves as an indication to Spring during the component scan that this instance should be created as a bean that will be available for use and injection into other beans in the application.

- The `CrudRepository` interface defines the basic common methods to read, create, update, and delete data from a data repository. The extra methods that we will define in our `BookRepository` extension, `public Book findBookByIsbn(String isbn)`, indicate that Spring JPA should automatically translate the call to this method to a SQL finder query selecting a Book by its ISBN field. This is a convention-named mapping that translates the method name into a SQL query. It can be a very powerful ally, allowing you to build queries such as `findByNameIgnoringCase(String name)` and others.

- The `@Id` and `@GeneratedValue` annotations provide you with an indication that an annotated field should be mapped to a primary key column in the database and the value for this field should be generated, instead of being explicitly entered.

- The `@ManyToOne` and `@ManyToMany` annotations define the relational field associations that refer to the data stored in the other tables. In our case, multiple `Books` belong to one `Author` and many `Reviewers` review multiple `Books`. The `mappedBy` attribute in `@OneToMany` annotation declaration defines a reverse association mapping. It indicates to Hibernate that the mapping source of truth is defined in the `Book` class, in the `author` or `publisher` fields. The `Books` references from within `Author` and `Publisher` classes are merely reverse associations.

 For more information about all the vast capabilities of Spring Data, visit `http://docs.spring.io/spring-data/data-commons/docs/current/reference/html/`.

Scheduling executors

Earlier in this chapter, we discussed how the command-line runners can be used as a place to start the scheduled executor thread pools in order to run the worker threads in intervals. While that is certainly a possibility, Spring provides you with a more concise configuration to achieve the same goal: `@EnableScheduling`.

Getting ready

We will enhance our application so that it will print a count of books in our repository every 10 seconds. To achieve this, we will make the necessary modifications to the `BookPubApplication` and `StartupRunner` classes.

How to do it...

1. Let's add an `@EnableScheduling` annotation to the `BookPubApplication` class, as follows:

```
@SpringBootApplication
@EnableScheduling
public class BookPubApplication {…}
```

2. As an `@Scheduled` annotation can be placed only on methods without arguments, let's add a new `run()` method to the `StartupRunner` class and annotate it with the `@Scheduled` annotation, as shown in the following line:

```
@Scheduled(initialDelay = 1000, fixedRate = 10000)
public void run() {
    logger.info("Number of books: " + bookRepository.count());
}
```

3. Start the application by executing `./gradlew clean bootRun` from the command line so as to observe the `Number of books: 0` message that shows in the logs every 10 seconds.

How it works...

Like some other annotations that we discussed in this chapter and will further discuss in the book, `@EnableScheduling` is not a Spring Boot annotation, but instead is a Spring Context module annotation. Similar to the `@SpringBootApplication` and `@EnableAutoConfiguration` annotations, this is a meta-annotation and internally imports the `SchedulingConfiguration` via the `@Import(SchedulingConfiguration.class)` instruction, which can be seen if looked found inside the code for the `@EnableScheduling` annotation class.

`ScheduledAnnotationBeanPostProcessor` that will be created by the imported configuration will scan the declared Spring Beans for the presence of the `@Scheduled` annotations. For every annotated method without arguments, the appropriate executor thread pool will be created. It will manage the scheduled invocation of the annotated method.

2

Configuring Web Applications

In the previous chapter, we learned how to create a starting application template, add some basic functionalities, and set up a connection to a database. In this chapter, we will continue to evolve our BookPub application and give it a web presence.

In this chapter, we will learn about the following topics:

- Creating a basic RESTful application
- Creating a Spring Data REST service
- Configuring custom servlet filters
- Configuring custom interceptors
- Configuring custom HttpMessageConverters
- Configuring custom PropertyEditors
- Configuring custom type Formatters

Creating a basic RESTful application

While command-line applications do have their place and use, most of today's application development is centered around web, REST, and data services. Let's start with enhancing our BookPub application by providing it with a web-based API in order to get access to the book catalogues.

We will start where we left off in the previous chapter, so there should already be an application skeleton with the entity objects and a repository service defined and a connection to the database configured.

How to do it...

1. The very first thing that we will need to do is add a new dependency to `build.gradle` with the `spring-boot-starter-web` starter to get us all the necessary libraries for a web-based functionality. The following snippet is what it would look like:

```
dependencies {
  compile("org.springframework.boot:spring-boot-starter-data-jpa")
  compile("org.springframework.boot:spring-boot-starter-jdbc")
  compile("org.springframework.boot:spring-boot-starter-web")
  runtime("com.h2database:h2")
  testCompile("org.springframework.boot:spring-boot-
    starter-test")
}
```

2. Next, we will need to create a Spring controller that will be used to handle the web requests for the catalog data in our application. Let's start by creating a new package structure to house our controllers so that we have our code nicely grouped by their appropriate purposes. Create a package folder called `controllers` in the `src/main/java/org/test/bookpub` directory from the root of our project.

3. As we will be exposing the Book data, let's create the controller class file called `BookController` in our newly created package with the following content:

```
@RestController
@RequestMapping("/books")
public class BookController {
  @Autowired
  private BookRepository bookRepository;

  @RequestMapping(value = "", method = RequestMethod.GET)
  public Iterable<Book> getAllBooks() {
    return bookRepository.findAll();
  }

  @RequestMapping(value = "/{isbn}", method =
    RequestMethod.GET)
  public Book getBook(@PathVariable String isbn) {
    return bookRepository.findBookByIsbn(isbn);
  }
}
```

4. Start the application by running `./gradlew clean bootRun`.

5. After the application has started, open the browser and go to `http://localhost:8080/books` and you should see a response: `[]`.

How it works...

The key to get the service exposed to web requests is the `@RestController` annotation. This is yet another example of a meta-annotation or a convenience annotation, as the Spring documentation refers to it at times, which we have seen in previous recipes. In `@RestController`, two annotations are defined: `@Controller` and `@ResponseBody`. So we could just as easily annotate `BookController`, as follows:

```
@Controller
@ResponseBody
@RequestMapping("/books")
public class BookController {...}
```

- ▸ `@Controller` is a Spring stereotype annotation that is similar to `@Bean` and `@Repository` and declares the annotated class as an MVC Controller

- ▸ `@ResponseBody` is a Spring MVC annotation indicating that responses from the web-request-mapped methods constitute the entire content of the HTTP response body payload, which is typical for RESTful applications

Creating a Spring Data REST service

In the previous example, we fronted our `BookRepository` with a REST controller in order to expose the data behind it via a web RESTful API. While this is definitely a quick and easy way to make the data accessible, it does require us to manually create a controller and define the mappings for all the desired operations. To minimize the boilerplate code, Spring provides us with a more convenient way: `spring-boot-starter-data-rest`. This allows us to simply add an annotation to the repository interface and Spring will do the rest to to expose it to the web.

We will continue from the place where we had finished in the previous recipe, and so the entity models and the `BookRepository` should already exist.

How to do it...

1. We will start by adding another dependency to our `build.gradle` file in order to add the `spring-boot-starter-data-rest` artefact:

```
dependencies {
    ...
    compile("org.springframework.boot:spring-boot-starter-data-rest")
    ...
}
```

2. Now, let's create a new interface to define `AuthorRepository` in the `src/main/java/org/test/bookpub/repository` directory from the root of our project with the following content:

```
@RepositoryRestResource
public interface AuthorRepository extends
    PagingAndSortingRepository<Author, Long> {
}
```

3. While we are at it—given how little code it takes—let's create the repository interfaces for the remaining entity models, `PublisherRepository` and `ReviewerRepository` by placing the files in the same package directory as `AuthorRepository` with the following content:

```
@RepositoryRestResource
public interface PublisherRepository extends
    PagingAndSortingRepository<Publisher, Long> {
}
```

Otherwise, you can use this code instead of the previous:

```
@RepositoryRestResource
public interface ReviewerRepository extends
    PagingAndSortingRepository<Reviewer, Long> {
}
```

4. Start the application by running `./gradlew clean bootRun`.

5. After the application has started, open the browser and go to
   `http://localhost:8080/authors` and you should see the following response:

```
localhost:8080/authors          ×

←  →  C  ⌂   □ localhost:8080/authors                    ⚡ ☆  ≡

{
  "_links" : {
    "self" : {
      "href" : "http://localhost:8080/authors{?page,size,sort}",
      "templated" : true
    }
  },
  "page" : {
    "size" : 20,
    "totalElements" : 0,
    "totalPages" : 0,
    "number" : 0
  }
}
```

How it works...

As is evident from the browser view, we will get significantly more information than
we got when we wrote the books controller. This is in part due to us extending not a
`CrudRepository` interface, but a `PagingAndSortingRepository` one, which in turn
is an extension of `CrudRepository`. The reason that we've decided to do this is to get the
extra benefits provided by the `PagingAndSortingRepository`. This will add the extra
functionality to retrieve entities using the pagination and being able to sort them.

The `@RepositoryRestResource` annotation, while optional, provides us with the ability to
have a finer control over the exposure of the repository as a web data service. For example,
if we wanted to change the URL path or `rel` value, to writers instead of `authors`, we could
have tuned the annotation, as follows:

```
@RepositoryRestResource(collectionResourceRel = "writers",
                        path = "writers")
```

As we included `spring-boot-starter-data-rest` in our build dependencies, we will
also get the `spring-hateoas` library support, which gives us nice ALPS metadata, such as a
`_links` object. This can be very helpful when building an API-driven UI, which can deduce the
navigational capabilities from the metadata and present them appropriately.

Configuring custom servlet filters

In a real-world web application, we almost always find a need to add facades or wrappers to service requests; to log them, filter out bad characters for XSS, perform authentication, and so on and so forth. Out of the box, Spring Boot automatically adds `OrderedCharacterEncodingFilter` and `HiddenHttpMethodFilter`, but we can always add more. Let's see how Spring Boot helps us achieve this task.

Among the various assortments of Spring Boot, Spring Web, Spring MVC, and others, there is already a vast variety of different servlet filters that are available and all we have to do is to define them as beans in the configuration. Let's say that our application will be running behind a load balancer proxy and we would like to translate the real request IP that is used by the users instead of the IP from the proxy when our application instance receives the request. Luckily, Tomcat 8 already provides us with an implementation: `RemoteIpFilter`. All we will need to do is add it to our filter chain.

How to do it...

1. It is a good idea to separate and group the configurations in different classes in order to provide more clarity about what kind of things are being configured. So, let's create a separate configuration class called `WebConfiguration` in the `src/main/java/org/test/bookpub` directory from the root of our project with the following content:

```
@Configuration
public class WebConfiguration {
  @Bean
  public RemoteIpFilter remoteIpFilter() {
    return new RemoteIpFilter();
  }
}
```

2. Start the application by running `./gradlew clean bootRun`.

3. In the startup log, we should see the following line, indicating that our filter has been added:

```
..FilterRegistrationBean  : Mapping filter: 'remoteIpFilter' to:
[/*]
```

How it works...

The magic behind this functionality is actually very simple. Let's start from the separate configuration class and work our way to the filter bean detection.

If we look in our main class, `BookPubApplication`, we will see that it is annotated with `@SpringBootApplication`, which in turn is a convenience meta-annotation that declares `@ComponentScan` among others. We discussed this in detail in one of our earlier recipes. The presence of `@ComponentScan` instructs Spring Boot to detect `WebConfiguration` as a `@Configuration` class and add its definitions to the context. So, anything that we will declare in `WebConfiguration` is as good as if we were to put it right in `BookPubApplication` itself.

The `@Bean public RemoteIpFilter remoteIpFilter() {…}` declaration simply creates a spring bean for the `RemoteIpFilter` class. When Spring Boot detects all the beans of `javax.servlet.Filter`, it will add them to the filter chain automatically. So, all we have to do, if we want to add more filters, is to just declare them as `@Bean` configurations. For example, for a more advanced filter configuration, if we want a particular filter to apply only to specific URL patterns, we can create a `@Bean` configuration of a `FilterRegistrationBean` type and use it to configure the precise settings.

Configuring custom interceptors

While Servlet Filters are a part of the Servlet API and have really nothing to do with Spring—besides being automatically added in the filter chain—Spring MVC provides us with another way of wrapping web requests: `HandlerInterceptor`. According to the documentation, `HandlerInterceptor` is just like a `Filter`; but instead of wrapping a request in a nested chain, an interceptor gives us cutaway points at different phases, such as before the request gets handled, after the request has been processed, before the view has been rendered, and at the very end, after the request has been fully completed. It does not let us change anything about the request but it does let us stop the execution by throwing an exception or returning false if the interceptor logic determines so.

Similar to the case with Filters, Spring MVC comes with a number of premade `HandlerInterceptors`. The commonly used ones are `LocaleChangeInterceptor` and `ThemeChangeInterceptor`; but there are certainly others that provide great value. So let's add `LocaleChangeInterceptor` to our application in order to see how it is done.

How to do it...

Despite what you might think, after seeing the previous recipe, adding an interceptor is not as straightforward as just declaring it a bean. We actually need to do it via `WebMvcConfigurer` or by overriding `WebMvcConfigurationSupport`.

1. Let's enhance our `WebConfiguration` class to extend `WebMvcConfigurerAdapter`:

   ```
   public class WebConfiguration extends
     WebMvcConfigurerAdapter {…}
   ```

2. Now we will add a @Bean declaration for LocaleChangeInterceptor:

```
@Bean
public LocaleChangeInterceptor localeChangeInterceptor() {
   return new LocaleChangeInterceptor();
}
```

3. This will actually create the interceptor spring bean but will not add it to the request handling chain. For this to happen, we will need to override the addInterceptors method and add our interceptor to the provided registry:

```
@Override
public void addInterceptors(InterceptorRegistry registry) {
   registry.addInterceptor(localeChangeInterceptor());
}
```

4. Start the application by running ./gradlew clean bootRun.

5. In the browser, go to http://localhost:8080/books?locale=foo.

6. Now, if you look at the console logs, you will see a bunch of stack trace errors basically saying the following:

```
Caused by: java.lang.UnsupportedOperationException: Cannot change
HTTP accept header - use a different locale resolution strategy
```

> The error is not because we entered an invalid locale, but because the default locale resolution strategy does not allow the resetting of the locale that is requested by the browser. The fact that we got an error shows that our interceptor is working.

How it works...

When it comes to configuring the Spring MVC internals, it is not as simple as just defining a bunch of beans—at least not always. This is due to the need of providing a more fine-tuned mapping of the MVC components to requests. To make things easier, Spring provides us with an adapter implementation of WebMvcConfigurer, WebMvcConfigurerAdapter, that we can extend and override the settings that we need.

In the particular case of configuring interceptors, we are overriding the addInterceptors(InterceptorRegistry registry) method. This is a typical callback method where we are given a registry in order to register as many additional interceptors as we need. During the MVC autoconfiguration phase, Spring Boot, just as in the case of Filters, detects instances of WebMvcConfigurer and sequentially calls the callback methods on all of them. It means that we can have more than one implementation of the WebMvcConfigurer class if we want to have some logical separation.

Configuring custom HttpMessageConverters

While we were building our RESTful web data service, we defined the controllers, repositories, and put some annotations on them; but nowhere did we do any kind of object translation from the java entity beans to the HTTP data stream output. However, behind the scenes, Spring Boot automatically configured `HttpMessageConverters` to translate our entity beans objects into a JSON representation using Jackson library, writing the resulting JSON data to an HTTP response output stream. When multiple converters are available, the most applicable one gets selected based on the message object class and the requested content type.

The purpose of `HttpMessageConverters` is to translate various object types into their corresponding HTTP output formats. A converter can either support a range of multiple data types or multiple output formats, or a combination of both. For example, `MappingJackson2HttpMessageConverter` can translate any Java Object into `application/json`, whereas `ProtobufHttpMessageConverter` can only operate on instances of `com.google.protobuf.Message` but can write them to the wire as `application/json`, `application/xml`, `text/plain`, or `application/x-protobuf`. `HttpMessageConverters` support not only writing out to the HTTP stream but also converting HTTP requests to appropriate Java objects as well.

How to do it...

There are a number of ways in which we can configure converters. It all depends on which one you prefer or how much control you want to achieve.

1. Let's add `ByteArrayHttpMessageConverter` as `@Bean` to our `WebConfiguration` class in the following manner:

```
@Bean
public
  ByteArrayHttpMessageConverter byteArrayHttpMessageConverter() {
    return new ByteArrayHttpMessageConverter();
}
```

2. Another way to achieve this is to override the `configureMessageConverters` method in the `WebConfiguration` class, which extends `WebMvcConfigurerAdapter`, defining such method as follows:

```
@Override
public void configureMessageConverters(
  List<HttpMessageConverter<?>> converters) {
    converters.add(new ByteArrayHttpMessageConverter());
}
```

3. If you want to have a bit more control, we can override the
`extendMessageConverters` method in the following way:

```
@Override
public void
  extendMessageConverters(List<HttpMessageConverter<?>>
    converters) {
  converters.clear();
  converters.add(new ByteArrayHttpMessageConverter());
}
```

How it works...

As you can see, Spring gives us multiple ways of achieving the same thing and it all depends on our preference or particular details of the implementation.

We covered three different ways of adding `HttpMessageConverter` to our application. So what is the difference, one might ask?

Declaring `HttpMessageConverter` as `@Bean` is the quickest and simplest way of adding a custom converter to the application. It is similar to how we added Servlet Filters in an earlier example. If Spring detects a bean of the `HttpMessageConverter` type, it will add it to the list automatically. If we did not have a `WebConfiguration` class that extends `WebMvcConfigurerAdapter`, it would have been the preferred approach.

When the application needs to dictate the extension of `WebMvcConfigurerAdapter` to configure other things such as interceptors, then it would be more consistent to override the `configureMessageConverters` method and add our converter to the list. As there can be multiple instances of `WebMvcConfigurers`, which could be either added by us or via the autoconfiguration settings from various Spring Boot Starters, there is no guarantee that our method can get called in any particular order.

If we need to do something even more drastic such as removing all the other converters from the list or clearing it of duplicate converters, this is where overriding `extendMessageConverters` comes into play. This method gets invoked after all the `WebMvcConfigurers` get called for `configureMessageConverters` and the list of converters is fully populated. Of course, it is entirely possible that some other instance of `WebMvcConfigurer` could override the `extendMessageConverters` as well; but the chances of this are very low so you have a high degree of having the desired impact.

Configuring custom PropertyEditors

In the previous example, we learned how to configure converters for an HTTP request and response data. There are other kinds of conversions that take place, especially in regards to dynamically converting parameters to various objects, such as Strings to Date or an Integer.

When we declare a mapping method in a controller, Spring allows us to freely define the method signature with the exact object types that we require. The way in which this is achieved is via the use of the `PropertyEditor` implementations. `PropertyEditor` is a default concept defined as part of the JDK and designed to allow the transformation of a textual value to a given type. It was initially intended to be used to build Java Swing/AWT GUI and later proved to be a good fit for Spring's need to convert web parameters to method argument types.

Spring MVC already provides you with a lot of `PropertyEditor` implementations for most of the common types, such as `Boolean`, `Currency`, and `Class`. Let's say that we want to create a proper `Isbn` class object and use this in our controller instead of a plain `String`.

How to do it...

1. First, we will need to remove the `extendMessageConverters` method from our `WebConfiguration` class as the `converters.clear()` call will break the rendering because we removed all of the supported type converters.

2. Next, we will add the definition of an `Isbn` object and `IsbnEditor` class as well as a method, `initBinder`, to our `BookController` where we will configure the `IsbnEditor` with the following content:

```
public class Isbn {
  private String isbn;

  public Isbn(String isbn) {
    this.isbn = isbn;
  }

  public String getIsbn() {
    return isbn;
  }
}

public class IsbnEditor extends PropertyEditorSupport {
  @Override
  public void setAsText(String text) throws
    IllegalArgumentException {
      if (StringUtils.hasText(text)) {
```

```
        setValue(new Isbn(text.trim()));
      }
      else {
        setValue(null);
      }
    }

    @Override
    public String getAsText() {
      Isbn isbn = (Isbn) getValue();
      if (isbn != null) {
        return isbn.getIsbn();
      }
      else {
        return "";
      }
    }
  }

  @InitBinder
  public void initBinder(WebDataBinder binder) {
    binder.registerCustomEditor(Isbn.class, new IsbnEditor());
  }
```

3. Our `getBook` method in the `BookController` will also change in order to accept the `Isbn` object, in the following way:

```
@RequestMapping(value = "/{isbn}", method = RequestMethod.GET)
public Book getBook(@PathVariable Isbn isbn) {
  return bookRepository.findBookByIsbn(isbn.getIsbn());
}
```

4. Start the application by running `./gradlew clean bootRun`.

5. In the browser, go to `http://localhost:8080/books/978-1-78528-415-1`.

6. While we will not observe any visible changes, the `IsbnEditor` is indeed at work, creating an instance of an `Isbn` class object from the `{isbn}` parameter.

How it works...

Spring automatically configures a large number of default editors; but for custom types, we have to explicitly instantiate new editors for every web request. This is done in the controller in a method that is annotated with `@InitBinder`. This annotation is scanned and all the detected methods should have a signature of accepting `WebDataBinder` as an argument. Among other things, `WebDataBinder` provides us with an ability to register as many custom editors as we require for the controller methods to be bound properly.

> It is **VERY** important to know that `PropertyEditor` is not thread safe! For this reason, we have to create a new instance of our custom editors for every web request and register them with `WebDataBinder`.

In case a new `PropertyEditor` is needed, it is best to create one by extending `PropertyEditorSupport` and overriding the desired methods with custom implementation.

Configuring custom type Formatters

Mostly because of its statefulness and lack of thread safety, since version 3, Spring has added a `Formatter` interface as a replacement for `PropertyEditor`. The Formatters are intended to provide a similar functionality but in a completely thread-safe manner and focusing on a very specific task of parsing a String in an object type and converting an object to its String representation.

Let's suppose that for our application, we would like to have a Formatter that would take an ISBN number of a book in a `String` form and convert it to a `Book` entity object. This way, we can define the controller request methods with a `Book` argument when the request URL signature only contains an ISBN number or a database ID.

How to do it...

1. First, let's create a new package called `formatters` in the `src/main/java/org/test/bookpub` directory from the root of our project.

2. Next, we will create the `Formatter` implementation called `BookFormatter` in our newly created `formatters` directory from the root of our project with the following content:

```
public class BookFormatter implements Formatter<Book> {
  private BookRepository repository;
  public BookFormatter(BookRepository repository) {
    this.repository = repository;
  }
```

```
@Override
public Book parse(String bookIdentifier, Locale locale)
    throws ParseException {
    Book book = repository.findBookByIsbn(bookIdentifier);
    return book != null ? book :
        repository.findOne(Long.valueOf(bookIdentifier));
}
@Override
public String print(Book book, Locale locale) {
    return book.getIsbn();
}
}
```

3. Now that we have our formatter, we will add it to the registry by overriding an `addFormatters(FormatterRegistry registry)` method in the `WebConfiguration` class:

```
@Autowired
private BookRepository bookRepository;
@Override
public void addFormatters(FormatterRegistry registry) {
    registry.addFormatter(new BookFormatter(bookRepository));
}
```

4. Finally, let's add a new request method to our `BookController` class located in the `src/main/java/org/test/bookpub/controllers` directory from the root of our project that will display the reviewers for a given ISBN of a book:

```
@RequestMapping(value = "/{isbn}/reviewers", method =
    RequestMethod.GET)
public List<Reviewer> getReviewers(@PathVariable("isbn") Book
book) {
    return book.getReviewers();
}
```

5. Just so that we can have some data to play with, let's manually (for now) populate our database with some test data by adding two more autowired repositories to the `StartupRunner` class:

```
@Autowired private AuthorRepository authorRepository;
@Autowired private PublisherRepository publisherRepository;
```

   ❑ The following code snippet is used for `StartupRunner`'s `run(...)` method:

```
Author author = new Author("Alex", "Antonov");
author = authorRepository.save(author);
Publisher publisher = new Publisher("Packt");
publisher = publisherRepository.save(publisher);
Book book = new Book("978-1-78528-415-1", "Spring Boot
Recipes", author, publisher);
bookRepository.save(book);
```

6. Start the application by running `./gradlew clean bootRun`.

7. Let's open `http://localhost:8080/books/978-1-78528-415-1/reviewers` in the browser and you should be able to see the following results:

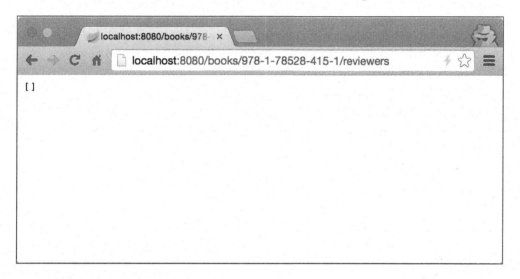

How it works...

The Formatter facility is aimed towards providing a similar functionality to `PropertyEditors`. By registering our formatter with the `FormatterRegistry` in the overridden `addFormatters` method, we are instructing Spring to use our Formatter to translate a textual representation of our `Book` into an entity object and back. As Formatters are stateless, we don't need to do the registration in our controller for every call; we have to do it only once and this will ensure Spring to use it for every web request.

> It is also good to remember that if you want to define a conversion of a common type, such as `String` or `Boolean`—as we did in our `IsbnEditor` example—it is best to do this via `PropertyEditors` initialization in Controller's `InitBinder` method because such a change is probably not globally desired and is only needed for a particular Controller's functionality.

You have probably noticed that we also autowired `BookRepository` to a `WebConfiguration` class, as this was needed to create the `BookFormatter`. This is one of the cool things about Spring—it lets us combine the configuration classes and make them dependent on the other beans at the same time. As we indicated that we need a `BookRepository` in order to create a `WebConfiguration` class, Spring ensured that the `BookRepository` will be created first and then automatically injected as a dependency during the creation of the `WebConfiguration` class. After `WebConfiguration` is instantiated, it is processed for configuration instructions.

The rest of the added functionalities should already be familiar as we covered that in our previous recipes. We will explore how to automatically populate databases with schemas and data in *Chapter 5, Application Testing*, in detail, where we will also talk about application testing.

3
Web Framework Behavior Tuning

In this chapter, we will learn about the following topics:

- ▶ Configuring route matching patterns
- ▶ Configuring custom static path mappings
- ▶ Tuning Tomcat via the EmbeddedServletContainerCustomizer
- ▶ Choosing embedded servlet containers
- ▶ Adding custom connectors

Introduction

In *Chapter 2, Configuring Web Applications*, we explored how to configure web applications in Spring Boot with our custom filters, interceptors, and so on. We will continue to look further into enhancing our web application by doing behavior tuning, configuring the custom routing rules and patterns, adding additional static asset paths, and adding and modifying servlet container connectors and other properties such as enabling SSL.

Configuring route matching patterns

When we build web applications, it is not always the case that a default, out-of-the-box, mapping configuration is applicable. At times, we want to create our RESTful URLs that contain characters such as . (dot), which Spring treats as a delimiter defining format, for example the dot in `path.xml`, or we might not want to recognize a trailing slash, as in `/home/`, and so on. Conveniently, Spring provides us with a way to get this accomplished with ease.

In *Chapter 2, Configuring Web Applications*, we introduced a `WebConfiguration` class, which extends from `WebMvcConfigurerAdapter`. This extension allows us to override methods that are geared toward adding filters, formatters, and many more. It also has methods that can be overridden in order to configure the path match, among other things.

Let's imagine that the ISBN format does allow the use of dots to separate the book number from the revision with a pattern looking like `[isbn-number].[revision]`.

How to do it...

We will configure our application to not use the suffix pattern match of `.*` and not to strip the values after the dot when parsing the parameters. Let's perform the following steps:

1. Let's add the necessary configuration to our `WebConfiguration` class with the following content:

```
@Override
public void configurePathMatch(PathMatchConfigurer configurer) {
    configurer.setUseSuffixPatternMatch(false).
        setUseTrailingSlashMatch(true);
}
```

2. Start the application by running `./gradlew clean bootRun`.

3. Let's open `http://localhost:8080/books/978-1-78528-415-1.1/reviewers` in the browser to see the following results:

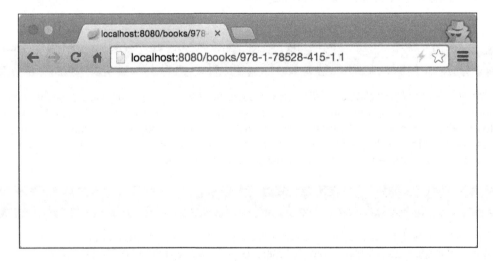

If we enter the correct ISBN, we will see a different result, as follows:

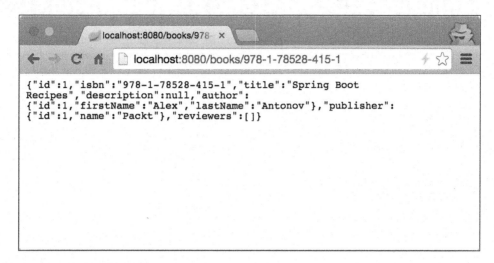

How it works...

Let's look at what we did in detail. The `configurePathMatch(PathMatchConfigurer configurer)` method gives us an ability to set our own behavior in how we want Spring to match the request URL path to the controller parameters:

▶ The `configurer.setUseSuffixPatternMatch(false)` method indicates that we don't want to use the `.*` suffix so as to strip the trailing characters after the last dot. This translates into Spring parsing out the entire `978-1-78528-415-1.1` as an `{isbn}` parameter for `BookController`. So `http://localhost:8080/books/978-1-78528-415-1.1` and `http://localhost:8080/books/978-1-78528-415-1` will become different URLs.

▶ The `configurer.setUseTrailingSlashMatch(true)` method indicates that we want to use the trailing `/` in the URL as a match as if it were not there. This effectively makes `http://localhost:8080/books/978-1-78528-415-1` the same as `http://localhost:8080/books/978-1-78528-415-1/`.

If you want to do further configuration of how the path matching takes place, you can provide your own implementation of `PathMatcher` and `UrlPathHelper`, but these would be required in the most extreme and custom-tailored situations and are not generally recommended.

Configuring custom static path mappings

In the previous recipe, we looked at how to tune the URL path mapping for requests and translate them into controller methods. It is also possible to control how our web application deals with static assets and the files that exist on the file system or are bundled in the deployable archive.

Let's say that we want to expose our internal `application.properties` file via the static web URL of `http://localhost:8080/internal/application.properties` from our application. To get started with this, proceed with the steps in the next section.

How to do it...

1. Let's add a new method, `addResourceHandlers`, to the `WebConfiguration` class with the following content:

```
@Override
public void addResourceHandlers(ResourceHandlerRegistry registry)
{
    registry.addResourceHandler("/internal/**")
        .addResourceLocations("classpath:/");
}
```

2. Start the application by running `./gradlew clean bootRun`.

3. Let's open `http://localhost:8080/internal/application.properties` in the browser to see the following results:

```
spring.datasource.url =
jdbc:h2:~/test;DB_CLOSE_DELAY=-1;DB_CLOSE_ON_EXIT=FALSE
spring.datasource.username = sa
spring.datasource.password =

# Hibernate
hibernate.show_sql: true
spring.jpa.hibernate.ddl-auto=create-drop
```

How it works...

The method that we overrode, `addResourceHandlers(ResourceHandlerRegistry registry)`, is another configuration method from `WebMvcConfigurer`, which gives us an ability to define custom mappings for static resource URLs and connect them with the resources on the file system or application classpath. In our case, we defined a mapping of anything that is being accessed via the / internal URL to be looked for in `classpath:/` of our application. (For production environment, you probably don't want to expose the entire classpath as a static resource!) So let's look at what we did in detail, as follows:

▶ The `registry.addResourceHandler("/internal/**")` methods adds a resource handler to the registry to handle our static resources and it returns a `ResourceHandlerRegistration` to us, which can be used to further configure the mapping in a chained fashion. The `/internal/**` string is a path pattern that will be used to match against the request URL using `PathMatcher`. We have seen how `PathMatcher` can be configured in the previous example, but by default an `AntPathMatcher` implementation is used. We can configure more than one URL pattern to be matched to a particular resource location.

▶ The `addResourceLocations("classpath:/")` method is called on the newly created instance of `ResourceHandlerRegistration` and it defines the directories where the resources should be loaded from. These should be valid file systems or classpath directories, and there can be more than one entered. If multiple locations are provided, they will be checked in the order in which they were entered.

We can also configure a caching interval for the given resource using the `setCachePeriod(Integer cachePeriod)` method.

Tuning Tomcat via EmbeddedServletContainerCustomizer

Spring Boot exposes many of the server properties that can be used to configure things such as PORT, SSL, and others by simply setting the values in `application.properties`. However, if we need to do any more complex tuning, Spring Boot provides us with an `EmbeddedServletContainerCustomizer` interface to programmatically define our configuration.

Even though the session timeout can be easily configured by setting the `server.session-timeout` property in `application.properties` to our desired value in seconds, we will do it using `EmbeddedServletContainerCustomizer` to demonstrate the functionality.

How to do it...

1. Let's say that we want our session to last for one minute. To make this happen, we will add an `EmbeddedServletContainerCustomizer` bean to our `WebConfiguration` class with the following content:

```
@Bean
public
  EmbeddedServletContainerCustomizer
    embeddedServletContainerCustomizer() {
      return new EmbeddedServletContainerCustomizer() {
        @Override
        public void
          customize(ConfigurableEmbeddedServletContainer
            container) {
              container.setSessionTimeout(1, TimeUnit.MINUTES);
          }
      };
  }
```

2. Just for the purpose of demonstration, we will ask the `request` object for the session by calling `getSession()` method, which will force its creation. To do this, we will add a new request mapping to our `BookController` class with the following content:

```
@RequestMapping(value = "/session", method = RequestMethod.GET)
public String getSessionId(HttpServletRequest request) {
  return request.getSession().getId();
}
```

3. Start the application by running `./gradlew clean bootRun`.

4. Let's open `http://localhost:8080/books/session` in the browser to see the following results:

If we wait for more than a minute and then reload this page, the session ID will change to a different one.

How it works...

The `EmbeddedServletContainerCustomizer` interface defines the `customize(Con figurableEmbeddedServletContainer container)` method. This is actually a nice convenience for those using Java 8 as we can just return a lambda rather than create an implementation of the class. In this case, it would look as follows:

```
public
  EmbeddedServletContainerCustomizer
    embeddedServletContainerCustomizer() {
      return (ConfigurableEmbeddedServletContainer container) -> {
        container.setSessionTimeout(1, TimeUnit.MINUTES);
      };
}
```

During the application startup, the Spring Boot autoconfiguration detects the presence of the customizer and invokes the `customize(...)` method, passing the reference to a servlet container. In our specific case, we actually get an instance of the `TomcatEmbeddedServletContainerFactory` implementation; but depending on the kind of servlet container that is used, such as Jetty, or Undertow, the implementation will vary.

Choosing embedded servlet containers

Despite Tomcat being the default embedded container in Spring Boot, we are not limited to only one. Spring Boot provides you with ready-to-use starters for Jetty and Undertow as well, so we have a choice of containers.

If we decide that we want to use Jetty as our servlet container, we will need to add a Jetty starter to our build file.

How to do it...

1. As Tomcat already comes as a transitive dependency of Spring Boot, we will need to exclude it from our build dependency tree by adding the following to `build.gradle`:

```
configurations {
  compile.exclude module: "spring-boot-starter-tomcat"
}
```

2. We will also need to add a compile dependency to our build dependencies on Jetty:

```
compile("org.springframework.boot:spring-boot-starter-jetty")
```

3. To fix the compiler errors, we will need to remove the bean declaration of Tomcat's `RemoteIpFilter` from our `WebConfiguration` class as the Tomcat dependency has been removed.

4. Start the application by running `./gradlew clean bootRun`.

5. If we now look at the console logs, we will see that our application is running in Jetty:

```
2015-03-29 --- o.eclipse.jetty.server.ServerConnector    : Started
ServerConn...

2015-03-29 ----.s.b.c.e.j.JettyEmbeddedServletContainer : Jetty
started on port(s) 8080 (http/1.1)
```

How it works...

The reason that this works is because of Spring Boot's autoconfiguration magic. We had to remove the Tomcat dependency from the build file in order to prevent a dependency collision between Tomcat and Jetty. Spring Boot does a conditional scan of the classes in the classpath and depending on what it detects, it determines which servlet container will be used.

If we look in the `EmbeddedServletContainerAutoConfiguration` class, we will see the following conditional code that checks for the presence of `Servlet.class`, `Server.class` and `Loader.class` from the Jetty package in order to determine if `JettyEmbeddedServletContainerFactory` should be used:

```
/**
 * Nested configuration if Jetty is being used.
 */
@Configuration
@ConditionalOnClass({ Servlet.class, Server.class, Loader.class})
@ConditionalOnMissingBean(value = EmbeddedServletContainerFactory.
class, search = SearchStrategy.CURRENT)
public static class EmbeddedJetty {

  @Bean
  public
    JettyEmbeddedServletContainerFactory
      jettyEmbeddedServletContainerFactory() {
        return new JettyEmbeddedServletContainerFactory();
  }
}
```

The `@ConditionalOnClass` annotation tells Spring Boot to use only the `EmbeddedJetty` configuration if Jetty's classes, namely `org.eclipse.jetty.server.Server` and `org.eclipse.jetty.util.Loader`, are present in the classpath.

Adding custom connectors

Another very common scenario in the enterprise application development and deployment is to run the application with two separate HTTP port connectors: one for HTTP and the other for HTTPS.

Getting ready

We will start by going back to using Tomcat; so for this recipe, we will undo the changes that we implemented in the previous example.

In order to create an HTTPS connector, we will need a few things; but most importantly, we will need to generate Certificate keystore that is used to encrypt and decrypt the SSL communication with the browser.

If you are using Unix or Mac, you can do it by running the following command:

```
$JAVA_HOME/bin/keytool -genkey -alias tomcat -keyalg RSA
```

On Windows, this could be achieved via the following code:

```
"%JAVA_HOME%\bin\keytool" -genkey -alias tomcat -keyalg RSA
```

During the creation of the keystore, you should enter the information that is appropriate to you, including passwords, name, and so on. For the purpose of this book, we will use the default password: `changeit`. Once the execution is complete, a newly generated keystore file will appear in your home directory under the name: `.keystore`.

 You can find more information about preparing the certificate keystore at `https://tomcat.apache.org/tomcat-8.0-doc/ssl-howto.html#Prepare_the_Certificate_Keystore`.

How to do it...

With the keystore creation complete, we will need to create a separate properties file in order to store our configuration for the HTTPS connector, such as port and others. After that, we will create a configuration property binding object and use it to configure our new connector. Perform the following steps;

1. First, we will create a new properties file named `tomcat.https.properties` in the `src/main/resources` directory from the root of our project with the following content:

   ```
   custom.tomcat.https.port=8443
   custom.tomcat.https.secure=true
   ```

```
custom.tomcat.https.scheme=https
custom.tomcat.https.ssl=true
custom.tomcat.https.keystore=${user.home}/.keystore
custom.tomcat.https.keystore-password=changeit
```

2. Next, we will create a nested static class named `TomcatSslConnectorProperties` in our `WebConfiguration` class with the following content:

```
@ConfigurationProperties(prefix = "custom.tomcat.https")
public static class TomcatSslConnectorProperties {
  private Integer port;
  private Boolean ssl= true;
  private Boolean secure = true;
  private String scheme = "https";
  private File keystore;
  private String keystorePassword;
  //Skipping getters and setters to save space, but we do need
them

    public void configureConnector(Connector connector) {
      if (port != null)
        connector.setPort(port);
      if (secure != null)
        connector.setSecure(secure);
      if (scheme != null)
        connector.setScheme(scheme);
      if (ssl!= null)
        connector.setProperty("SSLEnabled", ssl.toString());
      if (keystore!= null && keystore.exists()) {
        connector.setProperty("keystoreFile",
          keystore.getAbsolutePath());
        connector.setProperty("keystorePassword",
          keystorePassword);
      }
    }
  }
}
```

3. Now, we will need to add our newly created `tomcat.http.properties` file as a Spring Boot property source and enable `TomcatSslConnectorProperties` to be bound. This can be done by adding the following code right above the class declaration of the `WebConfiguration` class:

```
@Configuration
@PropertySource("classpath:/tomcat.https.properties")
```

```
@EnableConfigurationProperties(WebConfiguration.
TomcatSslConnectorProperties.class)
public class WebConfiguration extends
  WebMvcConfigurerAdapter {...}
```

4. Finally, we will need to create an `EmbeddedServletContainerFactory` Spring bean where we will add our HTTPS connector. We will do that by adding the following code to the `WebConfiguration` class:

```
@Bean
public
  EmbeddedServletContainerFactory
    servletContainer(TomcatSslConnectorProperties properties) {
      TomcatEmbeddedServletContainerFactory tomcat = new
        TomcatEmbeddedServletContainerFactory();
      tomcat.addAdditionalTomcatConnectors(
        createSslConnector(properties)
      );
      return tomcat;
}

private Connector
  createSslConnector(TomcatSslConnectorProperties
    properties) {
    Connector connector = new Connector();
    properties.configureConnector(connector);
    return connector;
}
```

5. Start the application by running `./gradlew clean bootRun`.

6. Let's open `https://localhost:8443/internal/tomcat.https.properties` in the browser to see the following results:

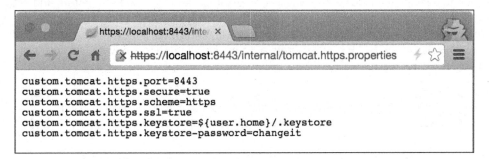

```
custom.tomcat.https.port=8443
custom.tomcat.https.secure=true
custom.tomcat.https.scheme=https
custom.tomcat.https.ssl=true
custom.tomcat.https.keystore=${user.home}/.keystore
custom.tomcat.https.keystore-password=changeit
```

How it works...

In this recipe, we did a number of things; so let's break them down one change at a time.

The first change, which we did in this recipe, ignoring the need to create the keystore, was the creation of `tomcat.https.properties` and `TomcatSslConnectorProperties` object to bind them to. Previously, we already dealt with making changes to the various settings in `application.properties` when configuring our DataSource. At that time, though, we did not have to create any binding objects because Spring Boot already has them defined.

As we learned earlier, Spring Boot already exposes many properties to configure the application settings, including a whole set of settings for the server configuration. These values get bound to an internal Spring Boot class: `ServerProperties`.

 A complete list of the common application properties can be found in the Spring Boot reference documentation at `http://docs.spring.io/spring-boot/docs/current/reference/html/common-application-properties.html`.

What we did with our addition was simply mimicking Spring Boot and creating our own configuration group with a binding object behind it. The reason that we didn't use the already existing `server.` prefix, and instead opted for `custom.tomcat`, was due to `ServerProperties` forbidding the reuse of the namespace and throwing an exception during property binding upon detection of unknown configuration fields, as it would have been in our case.

The `@ConfigurationProperties(prefix = "custom.tomcat.https")` method is an important annotation for our `TomcatSslConnectorProperties` object. It tells Spring Boot to automatically bind the properties with the `custom.tomcat.https` prefix to fields that are declared in `TomcatSslConnectorProperties`. In order for the binding to take place—in addition to defining the fields in the class—it is very important to define the getters and setters as well. It is also worth mentioning that during the binding process, Spring will automatically try to convert the property values to their appropriate data types. For example, the value of `custom.tomcat.https.keystore` gets automatically bound to a private File keystore field object.

 The converters, which we learned about earlier, will also be used during the process of converting to custom-defined data types.

The next step is to tell Spring Boot to include the properties that are defined in `tomcat.https.properties` in the list of properties. This is achieved by adding `@PropertySource("classpath:/tomcat.https.properties")` next to `@Configuration` in the `WebConfiguration` class.

After the values are imported, we will need to tell Spring Boot to automatically create an instance of `TomcatSslConnectorProperties` for us to use. This is done by adding the following annotation next to `@Configuration`:

```
@EnableConfigurationProperties(WebConfiguration.TomcatSslConnector
    Properties.class)
```

After all the property support is set and done, we will proceed with the actual code to create a second connector. The creation of the `EmbeddedServletContainerFactory` bean provides Spring Boot with a factory to use in order to create the `EmbeddedServletContainer`. The convenient `configureConnector(Connector connector)` method, which we added to `TomcatSslConnectorProperties`, gives us a good place to encapsulate and consolidate all the settings that are needed to configure the newly created `Connector` instance.

4

Writing Custom Spring Boot Starters

In this chapter, we will cover the following topics:

- ▶ Understanding Spring Boot autoconfiguration
- ▶ Creating a custom Spring Boot autoconfiguration starter
- ▶ Configuring custom conditional bean instantiations
- ▶ Using custom @Enable* annotations to toggle configurations

Introduction

In the previous chapters, we did a lot of configuration, and even more autoconfiguration while developing our Spring Boot application. Now, it is time to take a look behind the scenes and find out the magic behind the Spring Boot autoconfiguration, and write some starters of our own as well.

This is a very useful capability to possess, especially for large software enterprises where the presence of a proprietary code is inevitable, and it is very helpful to be able to create internal custom starters that would automatically add some of the configuration or functionalities to the applications. Some likely candidates can be custom configuration systems, libraries, and configurations that deal with connecting to databases, using custom connection pools, http clients, servers, and so on. We will go through the internals of Spring Boot autoconfiguration, take a look at how new starters are created, explore conditional initialization and wiring of beans based on various rules, and see that annotations can be a powerful tool, which provides the consumers of the starters with more control over dictating what configurations should be used and where.

Understanding Spring Boot autoconfiguration

Spring Boot has a lot of power when it comes to bootstrapping an application and configuring it with exactly the things that are needed, all without much of the glue code that is required of us, the developers. The secret behind this power actually comes from Spring itself or rather from the Java Configuration functionality that it provides. As we add more starters as dependencies, more and more classes will appear in our classpath. Spring Boot detects the presence or absence of specific classes and based on this information, makes some decisions, which are fairly complicated at times, and automatically creates and wires the necessary beans to the application context.

Sounds simple, right?

In the previous recipes, we added a number of Spring Boot starters such as `spring-boot-starter-data-jpa`, `spring-boot-starter-web`, `spring-boot-starter-data-test`, and so on. We will use the same code that we finished in the previous chapter in order to see what actually happens during the application startup and the decisions that Spring Boot will make while wiring our application together.

How to do it...

1. Conveniently, Spring Boot provides us with an ability to get the `AUTO-CONFIGURATION REPORT` by simply starting the application with the `debug` flag. This can be passed to the application either as an environment variable, `DEBUG`, as a system property, `-Ddebug`, or as an application property, `--debug`.

2. Start the application by running `DEBUG=true ./gradlew clean bootRun`.

3. Now, if you look at the console logs, you will see a lot more information printed there that is marked with the DEBUG level log. At the end of the startup log sequence, we will see the `AUTO-CONFIGURATION REPORT` as follows:

```
=========================

AUTO-CONFIGURATION REPORT

=========================



Positive matches:

-----------------

...

DataSourceAutoConfiguration
```

```
        - @ConditionalOnClass classes found: javax.sql.
DataSource,org.springframework.jdbc.datasource.embedded.
EmbeddedDatabaseType (OnClassCondition)

    ...



Negative matches:
----------------

    ...

GsonAutoConfiguration
        - required @ConditionalOnClass classes not found: com.
google.gson.Gson (OnClassCondition)

    ...
```

How it works...

As you can see, the amount of information that is printed in the debug mode can be somewhat overwhelming; so I've selected only one example of positive and negative matches each.

For each line of the report, Spring Boot tells us why certain configurations have been selected to be included, what they have been positively matched on, or, for the negative matches, what was missing that prevented a particular configuration to be included in the mix. Let's look at the positive match report for DataSourceAutoConfiguration:

> ▶ The @ConditionalOnClass marker in parenthesis classes found tells us that Spring Boot has detected the presence of a particular class, specifically two classes in our case: javax.sql.DataSource and org.springframework.jdbc. datasource.embedded.EmbeddedDatabaseType.

> ▶ The OnClassCondition indicates the kind of matching that was used. This is supported by the @ConditionalOnClass and @ConditionalOnMissingClass annotations.

While OnClassCondition is the most common kind of detection, Spring Boot also uses many other conditions. For example, OnBeanCondition is used to check the presence or absence of specific bean instances, OnPropertyCondition is used to check the presence, absence, or a specific value of a property as well as any number of the custom conditions that can be defined using the @Conditional annotation and Condition interface implementations.

The negative matches show us a list of configurations that Spring Boot has evaluated, which means that they do exist in the classpath and were scanned by Spring Boot but didn't pass the conditions required for their inclusion. `GsonAutoConfiguration`, while available in the classpath as it is a part of the imported `spring-boot-autoconfigure` artifact, was not included because the required `com.google.gson.Gson` class was not detected as present in the classpath, thus failing the `OnClassCondition` presence check.

The implementation of the `GsonAutoConfiguration` file looks as follows:

```
@Configuration
@ConditionalOnClass(Gson.class)
public class GsonAutoConfiguration {

  @Bean
  @ConditionalOnMissingBean
  public Gson gson() {
    return new Gson();
  }

}
```

After looking at the code, it is very easy to make the connection between the conditional annotations and the report information that is provided by Spring Boot at the start time.

Creating a custom Spring Boot autoconfiguration starter

We have a high-level idea of the process by which Spring Boot decides which configurations to include in the formation of the application context. Now, let's take a stab at creating our own Spring Boot starter artifact, which we can include as an autoconfigurable dependency in our build.

In *Chapter 2, Configuring Web Applications*, you learned how to create database Repository objects. So, let's build a simple starter that will create another `CommandLineRunner` that will take the collection of all the `Repository` instances and print out the count of the total entries for each.

We will start by adding a child Gradle project to our existing project that will house the codebase for the starter artifact. We will call it `db-count-starter`.

How to do it...

1. We will start by creating a new directory named `db-count-starter` in the root of our project.

2. As our project has now become what is known as a `multiproject` build, we will need to create a `settings.gradle` configuration file in the root of our project with the following content:

```
include 'db-count-starter'
```

3. We should also create a separate `build.gradle` configuration file for our subproject in the `db-count-starter` directory in the root of our project with the following content:

```
apply plugin: 'java'

repositories {
  mavenCentral()
  maven { url "https://repo.spring.io/snapshot" }
  maven { url "https://repo.spring.io/milestone" }

}

dependencies {
  compile("org.springframework.boot:spring-boot:1.2.3.RELEASE")
  compile("org.springframework.data:spring-data-
    commons:1.9.2.RELEASE")
}
```

4. Now we are ready to start coding. So, the first thing is to create the directory structure, `src/main/java/org/test/bookpubstarter/dbcount`, in the `db-count-starter` directory in the root of our project.

5. In the newly created directory, let's add our implementation of the `CommandLineRunner` file named `DbCountRunner.java` with the following content:

```
public class DbCountRunner implements CommandLineRunner {
    protected final Log logger = LogFactory.getLog(getClass());

    private Collection<CrudRepository> repositories;

    public DbCountRunner(Collection<CrudRepository>
      repositories) {
        this.repositories = repositories;
    }

    @Override
```

```
        public void run(String... args) throws Exception {
            repositories.forEach(crudRepository ->
                logger.info(String.format("%s has %s entries",
                    getRepositoryName(crudRepository.getClass()),
                    crudRepository.count()))));

        }


        private static String getRepositoryName(Class
    crudRepositoryClass) {
            for(Class repositoryInterface :
                    crudRepositoryClass.getInterfaces()) {
                if (repositoryInterface.getName().
    startsWith("org.test.bookpub.repository")) {
                    return repositoryInterface.getSimpleName();
                }
            }
            return "UnknownRepository";
        }
    }
```

6. With the actual implementation of DbCountRunner in place, we will now need to create the configuration object that will declaratively create an instance during the configuration phase. So, let's create a new class file called DbCountAutoConfiguration.java with the following content:

```
@Configuration
public class DbCountAutoConfiguration {
    @Bean
    public DbCountRunner dbCountRunner(
      Collection<CrudRepository> repositories) {
        return new DbCountRunner(repositories);
    }
}
```

7. We will also need to tell Spring Boot that our newly created JAR artifact contains the autoconfiguration classes. For this, we will need to create a resources/META-INF directory in the db-count-starter/src/main directory in the root of our project.

8. In this newly created directory, we will place the file named spring.factories with the following content:

```
org.springframework.boot.autoconfigure.
EnableAutoConfiguration=org.test.bookpubstarter.dbcount.
DbCountAutoConfiguration
```

9. For the purpose of our demo, we will add the dependency to our starter artifact in the main project's `build.gradle` by adding the following entry in the dependencies section:

```
compile project(':db-count-starter')
```

10. Start the application by running `./gradlew clean bootRun`.

11. Once the application is complied and has started, we should see the following in the console logs:

```
2015-04-05 INFO org.test.bookpub.StartupRunner          : Welcome
to the Book Catalog System!

2015-04-05 INFO o.t.b.dbcount.DbCountRunner              :
AuthorRepository has 1 entries

2015-04-05 INFO o.t.b.dbcount.DbCountRunner              :
PublisherRepository has 1 entries

2015-04-05 INFO o.t.b.dbcount.DbCountRunner              :
BookRepository has 1 entries

2015-04-05 INFO o.t.b.dbcount.DbCountRunner              :
ReviewerRepository has 0 entries

2015-04-05 INFO org.test.bookpub.BookPubApplication  : Started
BookPubApplication in 8.528 seconds (JVM running for 9.002)

2015-04-05 INFO org.test.bookpub.StartupRunner          : Number
of books: 1
```

How it works...

Congratulations! You have now built your very own Spring Boot autoconfiguration starter.

First, let's quickly walk through the changes that we made to our Gradle build configuration and then we will examine the starter setup in detail.

As the Spring Boot starter is a separate, independent artifact, just adding more classes to our existing project source tree would not really demonstrate much. To make this separate artifact, we had a few choices: making a separate Gradle configuration in our existing project or creating a completely separate project altogether. The most ideal solution, however, was to just convert our build to Gradle Multi-Project Build by adding a nested project directory and subproject dependency to `build.gradle` of the root project. By doing this, Gradle actually creates a separate artifact JAR for us but we don't have to publish it anywhere, only include it as a compile `project(':db-count-starter')` dependency.

 For more information about Gradle multi-project builds, you can check out the manual at `http://gradle.org/docs/ current/userguide/multi_project_builds.html`.

Spring Boot Auto-Configuration Starter is nothing more than a regular Spring Java Configuration class annotated with the `@Configuration` annotation and the presence of `spring.factories` in the classpath in the `META-INF` directory with the appropriate configuration entries.

During the application startup, Spring Boot uses `SpringFactoriesLoader`, which is a part of Spring Core, in order to get a list of the Spring Java Configurations that are configured for the `org.springframework.boot.autoconfigure.EnableAutoConfiguration` property key. Under the hood, this call collects all the `spring.factories` files located in the `META-INF` directory from all the jars or other entries in the classpath and builds a composite list to be added as application context configurations. In addition to the `EnableAutoConfiguration` key, we can declare the following other keys with implementations, which would be automatically initializable during startup in a similar fashion:

> ▸ `org.springframework.context.ApplicationContextInitializer`
>
> ▸ `org.springframework.context.ApplicationListener`
>
> ▸ `org.springframework.boot.SpringApplicationRunListener`
>
> ▸ `org.springframework.boot.env.PropertySourceLoader`
>
> ▸ `org.springframework.boot.autoconfigure.template.TemplateAvailabilityProvider`
>
> ▸ `org.springframework.test.contex.TestExecutionListener`

Ironically enough, a Spring Boot Starter does not need to depend on the Spring Boot library as its compile time dependency. If we look at the list of class imports in the `DbCountAutoConfiguration` class, we will not see anything from the `org.springframework.boot` package. The only reason that we have a dependency declared on Spring Boot is because our implementation of `DbCountRunner` implements the `org.springframework.boot.CommandLineRunner` interface.

Configuring custom conditional bean instantiations

In the previous example, you learned how to get the basic Spring Boot Starter going. On the inclusion of the jar in the application classpath, the `DbCountRunner` bean will be created automatically and added to the application context. In the very first recipe of this chapter, we have also seen that Spring Boot has an ability to do conditional configurations depending on a few conditions, such as the presence of specific classes in the classpath, existence of a bean, and others.

For this recipe, we will enhance our starter with a conditional check. This will create the instance of `DbCountRunner` only if no other bean instance of this class has already been created and added to the application context.

How to do it...

1. In the `DbCountAutoConfiguration` class, we will add an `@ConditionalOnMissingBean` annotation to the `dbCountRunner(...)` method, as follows:

```
@Bean
@ConditionalOnMissingBean
public DbCountRunner
  dbCountRunner(Collection<CrudRepository> repositories) {
  return new DbCountRunner(repositories);
}
```

2. We will also need to add a dependency on the `spring-boot-autoconfigure` artifact to the dependencies section of the `db-count-starter/build.gradle` file:

```
compile("org.springframework.boot:spring-boot-
  autoconfigure:1.2.3.RELEASE")
```

3. Now, let's start the application by running `./gradlew clean bootRun` in order to verify that we will still see the same output in the console logs as we did in the previous recipe.

4. If we start the application with the `DEBUG` switch so as to see the `Auto-Configuration Report`, which we already learned in the first recipe of this chapter, we will see that our autoconfiguration is in the `Positive Matches` group, as follows:

DbCountAutoConfiguration#dbCountRunner

- @ConditionalOnMissingBean (types: org.test.bookpubstarter. dbcount.DbCountRunner; SearchStrategy: all) found no beans (OnBeanCondition)

5. Let's explicitly/manually create an instance of `DbCountRunner` in our main `BookPubApplication` configuration class and we will also override its `run(...)` method, just so we can see the difference in the logs:

```
protected final Log logger = LogFactory.getLog(getClass());
@Bean
public DbCountRunner
  dbCountRunner(Collection<CrudRepository> repositories) {
  return new DbCountRunner(repositories) {
    @Override
    public void run(String... args) throws Exception {
      logger.info("Manually Declared DbCountRunner");
    }
  };
}
```

6. Start the application by running `DEBUG=true ./gradlew clean bootRun`.

7. If we look at the console logs, we will see two things: the `Auto-Configuration Report` will print our autoconfiguration in the `Negative Matches` group and, instead of the count output for each repository, we will see `Manually Declared DbCountRunner`:

```
DbCountAutoConfiguration#dbCountRunner

    - @ConditionalOnMissingBean (types: org.test.bookpubstarter.
dbcount.DbCountRunner; SearchStrategy: all) found the following
[dbCountRunner] (OnBeanCondition)


2015-04-05 INFO org.test.bookpub.BookPubApplication$1    :
Manually Declared DbCountRunner
```

How it works...

As we learned from the previous recipe, Spring Boot will automatically process all the configuration class entries from `spring.factories` during the application context creation. Without any extra guidance, everything that is annotated with an `@Bean` annotation will be used to create a Spring Bean. This functionality is actually a part of the plain old Spring framework Java Configuration. To enhance this even further, Spring Boot adds an ability to conditionally control the rules for when certain `@Configuration` or `@Bean` annotations should be executed and when it is best to ignore them.

In our case, we used the `@ConditionalOnMissingBean` annotation to instruct Spring Boot to create our `DbCountRunner` bean only if there is no other bean matching either the class type or bean name already declared elsewhere. As we explicitly created an `@Bean` entry for `DbCountRunner` in the `BookPubApplication` configuration, this took precedence and caused `OnBeanCondition` to detect the existence of the bean; thus instructing Spring Boot not to use `DbCountAutoConfiguration` during the application context setup.

Using custom @Enable* annotations to toggle configurations

Allowing Spring Boot to automatically evaluate the classpath and detected configurations that are found there makes it very quick and easy to get a simple application going. However, there are times when we want to provide the configuration classes but require consumers of the starter library to explicitly enable such a configuration rather than relying on Spring Boot to decide automatically if it should be included or not.

We will modify our previous recipe to enable the starter via a meta-annotation rather than using the `spring.factories` route.

How to do it...

1. First, we will comment out the content of the spring.factories file located in db-count-starter/src/main/resources in the root of our project, as follows:

```
#org.springframework.boot.autoconfigure.EnableAutoConfiguration =\
#org.test.bookpubstarter.dbcount.DbCountAutoConfiguration
```

2. Next, we will need to create the meta-annotation. We will create a new file named EnableDbCounting.java in the db-count-starter/src/main/java/org/test/bookpubstarter/dbcount directory in the root of our project with the following content:

```
@Target(ElementType.TYPE)
@Retention(RetentionPolicy.RUNTIME)
@Import(DbCountAutoConfiguration.class)
@Documented
public @interface EnableDbCounting {
}
```

3. We will now add the @EnableDbCounting annotation to our BookPubApplication class and also remove the dbCountRunner(...) method from it, as shown in the following snippet:

```
@SpringBootApplication
@EnableScheduling
@EnableDbCounting
public class BookPubApplication {

  public static void main(String[] args) {
    SpringApplication.run(BookPubApplication.class, args);
  }

  @Bean
  public StartupRunner schedulerRunner() {
    return new StartupRunner();
  }
}
```

4. Start the application by running ./gradlew clean bootRun.

How it works...

After running the application, the first thing that you might have noticed is that the printed counts all showed 0, even though `StartupRunner` had printed `Number of books: 1` to the console, as shown in the following output:

```
o.t.b.dbcount.DbCountRunner              : AuthorRepository has 0 entries

o.t.b.dbcount.DbCountRunner              : BookRepository has 0 entries

o.t.b.dbcount.DbCountRunner              : PublisherRepository has 0
entries

o.t.b.dbcount.DbCountRunner              : ReviewerRepository has 0
entries

org.test.bookpub.StartupRunner           : Welcome to the Book Catalog
System!

org.test.bookpub.StartupRunner           : Number of books: 1
```

This is because Spring Boot is randomly executing `CommandLineRunners` and, as we changed the configuration to use the `@EnableDbCounting` annotation, it gets processed before the configuration in the `BookPubApplication` class itself. As the database population is done by us in the `StartupRunner.run(...)` method and the execution of `DbCountRunner.run(...)` happens before this, the database tables have no data and so report the `0` count.

If we want to enforce the order, Spring provides us with this ability using the `@Order` annotation. Let's annotate the `StartupRunner` class with `@Order(Ordered.LOWEST_PRECEDENCE - 15)`. As `LOWEST_PRECEDENCE` is the default order that is assigned, we will ensure that `StartupRunner` will be executed after `DbCountRunner` by slightly reducing the order number. Let's run the app again and now we will see that the counts are properly displayed.

Now that this little ordering issue is behind us, let's examine what we did with the `@EnableDbCounting` annotation in a bit more detail.

Without `spring.factories` containing the configuration, Spring Boot does not really know that the `DbCountAutoConfiguration` class should be included during the application context creation. By default, the configuration component scan will look only from the package to which `BookPubApplication` class belongs to and below, so anything that provides configuration and resides under `org.test.bookpub.*` will get detected and evaluated. As the packages for `BookPubApplication` and `DbCountAutoConfiguration` classes are different—`org.test.bookpub` versus `org.test.bookpubstarter.dbcount`—the scanner won't pick it up.

This is where our newly created meta-annotation comes into play. In the `@EnableDbCounting` annotation, there is a key nested annotation, `@Import(DbCountAutoConfiguration.class)`, which makes things happen. This is an annotation that is provided by Spring, which can be used to annotate other annotations with declarations of which configuration classes should be imported in the process. By annotating our `BookPubApplication` class with `@EnableDbCounting`, we transitively tell Spring that it should include `DbCountAutoConfiguration` as a part of the application context as well.

Using the convenience meta-annotations, `spring.factories`, and conditional bean annotations, we can now create sophisticated and elaborate custom autoconfiguration Spring Boot starters in order to solve the needs of our enterprises.

5

Application Testing

In this chapter, we will cover the following topics:

- ▶ Creating tests for MVC Controllers
- ▶ Automatically configuring database schema and populating it with data
- ▶ Creating tests using in-memory database with data fixtures
- ▶ Creating tests using Mockito to mock DB
- ▶ Writing tests using Cucumber
- ▶ Writing tests using Spock

Introduction

In the previous chapters we did a lot of coding. We created a new Spring Boot application from scratch, added an MVC component to it, some database services, made a few tweaks to the application behavior, and even wrote our very own Spring Boot Starter. It is now time to take the next step and learn what kind of tools and capabilities Spring Boot offers when it comes to testing all this code and how well it integrates with the other popular testing frameworks.

We will see how to use the Spring JUnit integration to create unit tests. Next, we will explore the options of setting up the database with test data to test against it. We will then look to the Behavior Driven Development tools, Cucumber and Spock, and see how they integrate with Spring Boot.

Creating tests for Spring MVC Controllers

In the previous chapters, we made a lot of progress in gradually creating our application; but how do we know that it actually does what we want it to do? More importantly, how do we know for sure that after six months, or even a year from now, it will still continue to do what we expected it to do at the very beginning? This question is best answered by creating a set of tests, preferably automated, that run a suite of assertions against our code. This ensures that we constantly get the same and expected outputs given the specific inputs. Having tests gives us the much needed peace of mind that our application is not only elegantly coded and looks beautiful, but it also performs reliably and is as much error free as possible.

In *Chapter 4, Writing Custom Spring Boot Starters*, we left off with our web application fitted with a custom-written Spring Boot starter. We will now create some basic tests to test our web application to ensure that all the controllers expose the expected RESTful URLs on which we can rely on as the service API. This type of testing is a bit beyond what is commonly known as **Unit Testing** as it tests the entire web application, requires the application context to be fully initialized, and all the beans should be wired together in order to work. This kind of testing is sometimes referred as **Integration** or **Service Testing**.

How to do it...

Spring Boot gets us going by already creating a placeholder test file, `BookPubApplicationTests.java`, in the `src/test/java/org/test/bookpub` directory at the root of our project with the following content:

```
@RunWith(SpringJUnit4ClassRunner.class)
@SpringApplicationConfiguration(classes = BookPubApplication.class)
public class BookPubApplicationTests {

  @Test
  public void contextLoads() {
  }

}
```

1. In `build.gradle`, we also get a test dependency on `spring-boot-starter-test`, as follows:

   ```
   testCompile("org.springframework.boot:spring-boot-starter-test")
   ```

2. We will go ahead and extend the basic template test to contain the following code:

   ```
   import static org.hamcrest.Matchers.containsString;
   import static org.junit.Assert.assertEquals;
   import static org.junit.Assert.assertNotNull;
   ```

```java
import static org.springframework.test.web.servlet.request.
MockMvcRequestBuilders.get;
import static org.springframework.test.web.servlet.result.
MockMvcResultMatchers.content;
import static org.springframework.test.web.servlet.result.
MockMvcResultMatchers.jsonPath;
import static org.springframework.test.web.servlet.result.
MockMvcResultMatchers.status;

@RunWith(SpringJUnit4ClassRunner.class)
@SpringApplicationConfiguration(classes = BookPubApplication.
class)
@WebIntegrationTest("server.port:0")
public class BookPubApplicationTests {
  @Autowired
  private WebApplicationContext context;
  @Autowired
  private BookRepository repository;
  @Value("${local.server.port}")
  private int port;

  private MockMvc mockMvc;
  private RestTemplate restTemplate = new TestRestTemplate();

  @Before
  public void setupMockMvc() {
    mockMvc = MockMvcBuilders.webAppContextSetup(context).build();
  }

  @Test
  public void contextLoads() {
    assertEquals(1, repository.count());
  }

  @Test
  public void webappBookIsbnApi() {
    Book book =
      restTemplate.getForObject("http://localhost:" +
        port + "/books/978-1-78528-415-1", Book.class);
    assertNotNull(book);
    assertEquals("Packt", book.getPublisher().getName());
  }
```

```
@Test
public void webappPublisherApi() throws Exception {
  mockMvc.perform(get("/publishers/1")).
    andExpect(status().isOk()).andExpect(content().
      contentType(MediaType.parseMediaType(
        "application/hal+json"))).
    andExpect(content().string(containsString("Packt"))).
    andExpect(jsonPath("$.name").value("Packt"));
  }
}
```

3. In order to be able to use the `jsonPath(…)` matcher at runtime, we will also need to add the following dependency to the `dependencies {…}` block in our `build.gradle` file:

```
testRuntime("com.jayway.jsonpath:json-path")
```

4. Execute the tests by running `./gradlew clean test`.

5. By the console output, we can tell that our tests have succeeded and are running, but we don't really see much information besides the following lines (truncated for brevity):

```
:compileJava
```

```
:compileTestJava
```

```
:testClasses
```

```
:test
```

```
2015-04-13 21:40:44.694  INFO 25739 --- [        Thread-4]
ationConfigEmbeddedWebApplicationContext : Closing org.
springframework.boot.context.embedded.AnnotationConfigEmbeddedWeb
ApplicationContext@206f4aa6: startup date [Mon Apr 13 21:40:36 CDT
2015]; root of context hierarchy
```

```
2015-04-13 21:40:44.704  INFO 25739 --- [        Thread-4]
j.LocalContainerEntityManagerFactoryBean : Closing JPA
EntityManagerFactory for persistence unit 'default'
```

```
2015-04-13 21:40:44.705  INFO 25739 --- [        Thread-4] org.
hibernate.tool.hbm2ddl.SchemaExport  : HHH000227: Running hbm2ddl
schema export
```

```
2015-04-13 21:40:44.780  INFO 25739 --- [        Thread-4] org.
hibernate.tool.hbm2ddl.SchemaExport  : HHH000230: Schema export
complete
```

```
BUILD SUCCESSFUL
```

```
Total time: 24.635 secs
```

6. A better insight can be gathered by viewing the HTML reports that are generated by Gradle, which can be opened in the browser and reside in `build/reports/tests/index.html`, as shown in the following screenshot:

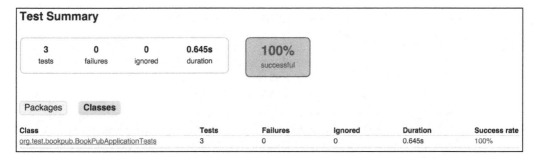

7. Clicking on `org.test.bookpub.BookPubApplicationTests` will take us to the individual test case breakdown that shows the status of each test and how long it took to get executed, as follows:

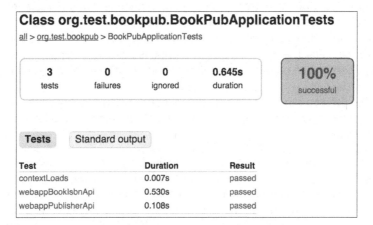

8. The more curious minds can also click on the **Standard output** button in order to see the runtime application logs that are produced during the execution of the test.

How it works...

Now that we created our first test, let's examine the code in detail.

We will first look at the following annotations that have been declared for the `BookPubApplicationTests` class:

- ▶ `@RunWith(SpringJUnit4ClassRunner.class)`: This is a standard JUnit annotation that we can configure so as to use the `SpringJUnit4ClassRunner` providing functionality of Spring Test Context framework to the standard JUnit tests.

- ▶ `@SpringApplicationConfiguration(classes = BookPubApplication.class)`: This is a Spring Boot annotation that is used to determine how to load and configure the Spring Application Context for the integration tests. It is a meta-annotation that contains the `ContextConfiguration` annotation, which instructs the testing framework to use Spring Boot's `SpringApplicationContextLoader` for application context creation.

- ▶ `@WebIntegrationTest("server.port:0")`: This is an annotation that indicates to Spring Boot that the current test is an integration test and will require a complete context initialization and application startup, as if it were a real deal. This annotation is usually included along with `@SpringApplicationConfiguration` for the integration tests. The `server.port:0` value is used to tell Spring Boot to start the Tomcat server on a randomly chosen http port, which we will later obtain by declaring the `@Value("${local.server.port}") private int port;` value field. This ability to select a random http port is very handy when running tests on a Jenkins or any other CI server where, if multiple jobs are running in parallel, you could get a port collision.

With the class annotations magic dispelled, let's look at the content of the class itself. As this is a Spring Boot test, we can declare any objects that are managed by Spring to be `@Autowired` during the execution or set to a specific environment value using an `@Value` annotation. In our test, we autowired the `WebApplicationContext` and `BookRepository` objects, which we will use in the execution of the standard JUnit `@Test` annotated test cases.

In the first test case, the `contextLoads()` method, we will just assert that we have the `BookRepository` connection established and that it contains our one book entry.

Our second test will ensure that our web application responds to a RESTful URL for a `Book` lookup by ISBN - `"/books/{isbn}"`. For this test, we will use the instance of `TestRestTemplate` and make a RESTful call to the running instance on a randomly selected port. Spring Boot provides the value of the `port` field.

Alternatively, we can execute the same flavor of tests by going through the `MockMvc` object. This is provided by the Spring Test framework and allows you to perform MVC testing without actually doing the client-side-based testing through `RestTemplate`, but instead doing it fully server-side where the Controller requests are executed from the same context as the tested application.

In order to use `MockMvc`, we will use the `MockMvcBuilders` utility to build an instance using `@Autowired WebApplicationContext`. We will do this in the setup method so that we don't have to do it in every test explicitly.

`MockMvc` provides us with a very extensive set of capabilities in order to execute assertions on practically all the things that are related to a web request. It is designed to be used in a method chained fashion, allowing us to link the various tests together and forming a nice continuous logical chain. We have used the following checks in our example:

- The `perform(get(…))` method sets up the web request. In our particular case, we perform a GET request but the `MockMvcRequestBuilders` class provides you with static helper functions for all the common method calls.

- The `andExpect(…)` method can be invoked multiple times where each call represents an evaluation of a condition against the result of the `perform(…)` call. The argument of this call is any implementation of the `ResultMatcher` interface along with many stock ones that are provided by the `MockMvcResultMatchers` static utility class. This really opens up a possibility of having an infinite number of different checks such as verifying the response status, content type, values stored in a session, flash scope, verify redirects, contents of the rendering model or headers, and much more. We will use a third-party `json-path` add-on library to test the JSON response data in order to ensure that it contains the right elements in the right tree hierarchy, `andExpect(jsonPath("$.name").value("Packt"))`, which validates that we have a name element at the root of the JSON document with a value of `Packt`.

> To learn more about the various possibilities that are available in `MockMvc`, you can refer to `https://github.com/spring-projects/spring-mvc-showcase/tree/master/src/test/java/org/springframework/samples/mvc`.

Automatically configuring the database schema and populating it with data

Earlier in the book, in *Chapter 2, Configuring Web Applications*, we manually added a few entries to the database in the `StartupRunner's run(...)` method. While doing so programmatically can be a quick and easy way to get something going very quickly, in the long run, it is not really a good idea to do so—especially when you are dealing with a large amount of data. It is also a good practice to separate the database preparations, changes, and other configurations from the rest of the running application code, even if it is setting up the test cases. Thankfully, Spring has provided you with the support to make this task fairly easy and straightforward to solve.

We will continue with the state of the application as we had left it in the previous recipe. Spring provides us with a couple of ways to define how both the structure and data should be populated in the database. The first way relies on using Hibernate to automatically create the table structure by inferring it from our defined `@Entity` objects and using the `import.sql` file to populate the data. The second approach is to use the plain old Spring JDBC capability, which relies on using the `schema.sql` file that contains the database table definition and a corresponding `data.sql` file that contains the data.

How to do it...

1. First, we will remove the programmatic database population, which we created in *Chapter 2. Configuring Web Applications*. So let's comment out the following code from the `StartupRunner's run(...)` method:

```
Author author = new Author("Alex", "Antonov");
author = authorRepository.save(author);
Publisher publisher = new Publisher("Packt");
publisher = publisherRepository.save(publisher);
Book book = new Book("978-1-78528-415-1", "Spring Boot Recipes",
author, publisher);
bookRepository.save(book);
```

2. If we were to run our tests, they might fail if the `test.h2.db` file is missing because they expect the data to be in the database. We will populate the database by creating a Hibernate `import.sql` file in the `src/main/resources` directory at the root of our project with the following content:

```
INSERT INTO author (id, first_name, last_name) VALUES (1, 'Alex',
'Antonov')
INSERT INTO publisher (id, name) VALUES (1, 'Packt')
INSERT INTO book (isbn, title, author_id, publisher_id) VALUES
('978-1-78528-415-1', 'Spring Boot Recipes', 1, 1)
```

3. On running the tests again by running `./gradlew clean test`, they are magically started to get passed again.

4. Another way to do this is to use the Spring JDBC support for `schema.sql` and `data.sql`. Let's rename the newly created `import.sql` file to `data.sql` and create a `schema.sql` file in the same directory with the following content:

```
-- Create syntax for TABLE 'author'
DROP TABLE IF EXISTS `author`;
CREATE TABLE `author` (
  `id` bigint(20) NOT NULL AUTO_INCREMENT,
  `first_name` varchar(255) DEFAULT NULL,
  `last_name` varchar(255) DEFAULT NULL,
  PRIMARY KEY (`id`)
);
-- Create syntax for TABLE 'publisher'
DROP TABLE IF EXISTS `publisher`;
CREATE TABLE `publisher` (
  `id` bigint(20) NOT NULL AUTO_INCREMENT,
  `name` varchar(255) DEFAULT NULL,
  PRIMARY KEY (`id`)
);
-- Create syntax for TABLE 'reviewer'
DROP TABLE IF EXISTS `reviewer`;
CREATE TABLE `reviewer` (
  `id` bigint(20) NOT NULL AUTO_INCREMENT,
  `first_name` varchar(255) DEFAULT NULL,
  `last_name` varchar(255) DEFAULT NULL,
  PRIMARY KEY (`id`)
);
-- Create syntax for TABLE 'book'
DROP TABLE IF EXISTS `book`;
CREATE TABLE `book` (
  `id` bigint(20) NOT NULL AUTO_INCREMENT,
  `description` varchar(255) DEFAULT NULL,
  `isbn` varchar(255) DEFAULT NULL,
  `title` varchar(255) DEFAULT NULL,
  `author_id` bigint(20) DEFAULT NULL,
  `publisher_id` bigint(20) DEFAULT NULL,
  PRIMARY KEY (`id`),
  CONSTRAINT `FK_publisher` FOREIGN KEY (`publisher_id`)
REFERENCES `publisher` (`id`),
```

```
    CONSTRAINT `FK_author` FOREIGN KEY (`author_id`) REFERENCES
`author` (`id`)
);
-- Create syntax for TABLE 'book_reviewers'
DROP TABLE IF EXISTS `book_reviewers`;
CREATE TABLE `book_reviewers` (
  `book_id` bigint(20) NOT NULL,
  `reviewers_id` bigint(20) NOT NULL,
  CONSTRAINT `FK_book` FOREIGN KEY (`book_id`) REFERENCES `book`
(`id`),
  CONSTRAINT `FK_reviewer` FOREIGN KEY (`reviewers_id`) REFERENCES
`reviewer` (`id`)
);
```

5. As we are now manually creating the database schema, we will need to tell the Hibernate mapper not to automatically derive one from the entities and populate the database with it. So, let's set the `spring.jpa.hibernate.ddl-auto=none` property in the `application.properties` file in the `src/main/resources` directory at the root of our project.

6. Execute the tests by running `./gradlew clean test` and they should get passed.

How it works...

In this recipe, we actually explored two ways of achieving the same thing and this is quite common when you are living in the Spring ecosystem. Depending on the components that are used, whether it's a plain Spring JDBC, Spring JPA with Hibernate, or the Flyway or Liquidbase migrations, the approach of populating and initializing the database differs but the end result remains pretty much the same.

 Both Flyway and Liquidbase are frameworks that provide incremental database migration capabilities. This comes in very handy when one wants to maintain the incremental log of the database changes in a programmatic, describable fashion with an ability to quickly put the database in a desired state for a particular version. While these frameworks differ in their approach of providing such support, they are similar in the purpose. More detailed information can be obtained at their respective sites, `http://flywaydb.org` and `http://www.liquibase.org`.

In the preceding example, we explored two different ways of populating and initializing the database.

Initializing the database with Spring JPA and Hibernate

In this approach, most of the work is actually done by the `Hibernate` library and we merely set up the appropriate configurations and create conventionally expected files that are needed for `Hibernate` to do the work. In this recipe we have used the following settings:

- The `spring.jpa.hibernate.ddl-auto=create-drop` setting instructs `Hibernate` to use the `@Entity` models and, based on their structure, automatically deduce the database schema. On starting the application, the calculated schema will be used to preinitialize the database table structure; when the application is shut down, it will all be destroyed. Even in the event where the application was forcefully terminated or it abruptly crashed, on startup, if the existing tables are detected, they will be dropped and recreated from scratch; so it's probably not a good idea to rely on this for the production environment.

> If the `spring.jpa.hibernate.ddl-auto` property is not explicitly configured, Spring Boot uses `create-drop` for embedded databases such as `H2` by default; so be careful and set it appropriately.

- The `import.sql` file is also expected to reside in the root of the classpath by `Hibernate`. This is used to execute the declared SQL statements on the application startup. While any valid SQL statement can go in the file, it is recommended that you put the data importing statements such as `INSERT` or `UPDATE` and stay clear of table structure mutations, as the schema definition is already taken care of by `Hibernate`.

Initializing the database with Spring JDBC

If the application does not use JPA or you don't want to depend on the Hibernate functionality explicitly, Spring offers you another way of getting the database set up, as long as the `spring-boot-starter-jdbc` dependency is present. So let's take a look at what we did to get it to work, as shown in the following list:

- The `spring.jpa.hibernate.ddl-auto=none` setting tells Hibernate not to do any automatic handling of the database if the Hibernate dependency also exists, as it does in our case. This setting is a good practice for the production environment as you probably don't want to get all of your database tables wiped out clean inadvertently—that would be one hell of a disaster, that's for sure!

▶ The `schema.sql` file is expected to exist in the root of the classpath. It is executed by Spring during the schema creation of the database on every startup of the application. However, unlike Hibernate, this will not drop any of the existing tables automatically, so it might be a good idea to either use `DROP TABLE IF EXISTS` to delete an existing table before creating the new one or use the `CREATE TABLE IF NOT EXISTS` as a part of the table creation SQL, if we only want to create new tables in case they don't already exist. This makes it a lot more flexible to declare the database structure evolution logic, thus making it safer to be used in production as well.

▶ The `data.sql` file is expected to exist in the root of the classpath. This is used to execute the data population SQL, so this is where all the `INSERT INTO` statements go.

Given that this is a Spring native functionality, we will also get the ability to define the schema and data files not only globally, but also as per the specific database platform. For example, we can have one set of files that we can use for Oracle, `schema-oracle.sql`, and a different one for MySQL, `schema-mysql.sql`. The same applies to the `data.sql` variants as well; however, they don't have to be all defined per platform, so while you might have platform-specific schema files, there could be a shared data file. The `spring.datasource.platform` configuration value can be explicitly set if you want to override Spring Boot's automatically deduced value.

If one wants to override the default names of `schema.sql` and `data.sql`, Spring Boot provides us with the configuration properties, which we can use to control `spring.datasource.schema` and `spring.datasource.data`.

Creating tests using in-memory database with data fixtures

In the previous recipe, we explored how to get our databases set up with the desired tables and populated with the needed data. When it comes to testing, one of the typical challenges is to get the environment set up correctly and predictably so that when the tests are executed, we can safely assert the behavior in a deterministic fashion. In an application that connects to a database, making sure that the database contains a deterministic dataset on which the assertions can be evaluated is extremely important. For an elaborate test suite, it is also necessary to be able to refresh or change that dataset based on the tests. Thankfully, Spring has some nice facilities that aid you in accomplishing this task.

We will pick up from the state of our `BookPub` application as we left it in the previous recipe. At this point, we have the `schema.sql` file defining all the tables and we also need the database with some starting data that is defined in `data.sql`. In this recipe, we will extend our tests to use the specific data fixture files that are tailored to a particular test suite.

How to do it...

1. Our first step will be to create a `resources` directory in the `src/test` directory at the root of our project.

2. In this directory, we will start placing our fixture SQL data files. Let's create a new file named `test-data.sql` in the resources directory with the following content:

```
INSERT INTO author (id, first_name, last_name) VALUES (2, 'Greg',
'Turnquist')
INSERT INTO book (isbn, title, author_id, publisher_id) VALUES
('978-1-78439-302-1', 'Learning Spring Boot', 2, 1)
```

3. We now need a way to load this file when our test runs. We will modify our `BookPubApplicationTests` class in the following way:

```
public class BookPubApplicationTests {
    ...
    @Autowired
    private BookRepository repository;
    @Autowired
    private DataSource ds;
    @Value("${local.server.port}")
    private int port;

    private MockMvc mockMvc;
    private RestTemplate restTemplate = new TestRestTemplate();
    private static boolean loadDataFixtures = true;

    @Before
    public void setupMockMvc() {
        ...
    }

    @Before
    public void loadDataFixtures() {
        if (loadDataFixtures) {
            ResourceDatabasePopulator populator = new ResourceDatabas
ePopulator(context.getResource("classpath:/test-data.sql"));
            DatabasePopulatorUtils.execute(populator, ds);
            loadDataFixtures = false;
        }
    }

    @Test
    public void contextLoads() {
```

```
        assertEquals(2, repository.count());
    }

    @Test
    public void webappBookIsbnApi() {
        ...
    }

    @Test
    public void webappPublisherApi() throws Exception {
        ...
    }
}
```

4. Execute the tests by running ./gradlew clean test and they should continue to get passed despite us adding another book and its author to the database.

5. We can also use the method of populating the database, which we have learned in the previous recipe. As the test code has its own resources directory, it is possible to add another data.sql file to it and Spring Boot will use both the files to populate the database. Let's go ahead and create the data.sql file in the src/test/resources directory at the root of our project with the following content:

```
INSERT INTO author (id, first_name, last_name) VALUES (3,
'William', 'Shakespeare')
INSERT INTO publisher (id, name) VALUES (2, 'Classical Books')
INSERT INTO book (isbn, title, author_id, publisher_id) VALUES
('978-1-23456-789-1', 'Romeo and Juliet', 3, 2)
```

 As Spring Boot collects all the occurrences of the data files from the classpath, it is possible to place the data files in JARs or different physical locations that all end up being at the root of the classpath.

 It is also important to remember that as the loading order of these scripts is not deterministic and in case you rely on certain referential IDs, it is better if you use selects to get them instead of making assumptions.

6. As we added another book to the database and now that we have three of them, we should fix the assertion in our contextLoads() test method to the following:

```
assertEquals(3, repository.count());
```

7. Execute the tests by running ./gradlew clean test and they should continue to pass.

8. It would be a fair statement that when running unit tests, an in-memory database is probably more suitable for the role as compared to a persistent one. Let's create a dedicated test configuration instance of the `application.properties` file in the `src/test/resources` directory at the root of our project with the following content:

    ```
    spring.datasource.url = jdbc:h2:mem:testdb;DB_CLOSE_DELAY=-1;DB_
    CLOSE_ON_EXIT=FALSE
    spring.jpa.hibernate.ddl-auto=none
    ```

> It is important to know that Spring Boot loads only one `application.properties` from the classpath. When we created another `application.properties` in `src/test/resources`, the previous one from `src/main/resources` was no longer loaded and thus none of the properties defined in here were merged in the environment. For this reason, you should configure all of the property values that are needed. In our case, we had to redefine the `spring.jpa.hibernate.dll-auto` property, even though it was already declared in `src/main/resources/application.properties`.

9. Execute the tests by running `./gradlew clean test` and the tests should continue to get passed.

How it works...

In this recipe, we relied on the facility that is provided by Spring to initialize and populate the database in order to get our database populated with the data needed to run the tests and assert on them; however, we also wanted to be able to use some data that is only relevant to a particular test suite. For this, we turned to the `ResourceDatabasePopulator` and `DatabasePopulatorUtils` classes to insert the desired data right before the test gets executed. These are exactly the same classes that are used internally by Spring in order to handle the `schema.sql` and `data.sql` files, except that now we are explicitly defining the script files that we want to execute.

So, let's break up what we did step by step, as follows:

▸ We created a setup method named `loadDataFixtures()`, which we annotated with an `@Before` annotation to tell JUnit to run it before every test.

▸ In this method, we obtained a resource handle to the `classpath:/test-data.sql` data file that resides in our application's classpath and where we store our test data and execute it against `@Autowired DataSource ds`.

▶ As Spring can only autowire dependencies in the instances of the class and the @Before annotated setup methods get executed for every test, we had to get a little creative in order to avoid repopulating our database with the duplicate data for every test instead of once per test suite/class. To achieve this, we created a static boolean loadDataFixtures variable that retains its state for every instance of the BookPubApplicationTests class, thus ensuring that we execute DatabasePopulatorUtils only once. The reason that the variable has to be static is as a new instance of the test class gets created for every test method that it runs in the class, having the boolean flag at the instance level will not do the trick.

▶ For a finishing touch, we decided to have a separate application.properties file to be used for testing purposes. We added this to our src/test/resources classpath with a testing configuration of the in-memory database instead of using the file-based persistent one.

Unlike application.properties where only one file can be loaded from the classpath, Spring supports a number of profile configurations, which will get all merged together, during the application startup. So, instead of declaring a completely separate application. properties file, we could create an application-test. properties file and set an active profile to test while running the tests.

Creating tests using Mockito to mock DB

Now that we are done with setting up the fixtures to use during the set up and population of our database when it is used for testing purposes, let's examine how we can use the power of Mockito so that we don't need to rely on the database at all. We will learn how to elegantly mock the Repository instance objects using the Mockito framework and some annotation cleverness.

We will create a special Spring Boot configuration class where we will define and replace the Spring Beans that are necessary for testing purposes. We will use annotations to tell Spring Boot when to add the testing configuration and when to exclude it. In the configuration class, we will use Mockito to create some mock objects with preconfigured behavior, which will later be injected by Spring Boot while executing the tests.

How to do it...

1. First, we will create a special annotation that we will use in order to tag the configuration classes that are designed to be loaded for testing purposes only. To achieve this, we will enhance our BookPubApplication class with the following content:

```
@Configuration
@EnableAutoConfiguration
@ComponentScan(excludeFilters=@ComponentScan.
Filter(UsedForTesting.class))
@EnableScheduling
@EnableDbCounting

public class BookPubApplication {

  public static void main(String[] args) {
    SpringApplication.run(BookPubApplication.class, args);
  }

  ...

}


@interface UsedForTesting {}
```

2. With this annotation defined, we are ready to create our TestMockBeansConfig class in the src/test/java/org/test/bookpub directory at the root of our project with the following content:

```
@Configuration
@UsedForTesting
public class TestMockBeansConfig {
  @Bean
  @Primary
  public PublisherRepository
    createMockPublisherRepository() {
    return Mockito.mock(PublisherRepository.class);
  }
}
```

3. We will also create a separate test suite class as we have too much going on already in the BookPubApplicationTests. Let's create a separate test file named PublisherRepositoryTests.java in the src/test/java/org/test/bookpub directory at the root of our project with the following content:

```
@RunWith(SpringJUnit4ClassRunner.class)
@SpringApplicationConfiguration(classes = {BookPubApplication.class,
   TestMockBeansConfig.class})
@IntegrationTest
public class PublisherRepositoryTests {
  @Autowired
  private PublisherRepository repository;

  @Before
  public void setupPublisherRepositoryMock() {
    Mockito.when(repository.count()).thenReturn(1L);
  }

  @Test
  public void publishersExist() {
    assertEquals(1, repository.count());
  }

  @After
  public void resetPublisherRepositoryMock() {
    Mockito.reset(repository);
  }
}
```

4. Execute the tests by running ./gradlew clean test and the tests should get passed.

How it works...

There are a few magical things happening here. Let's start with the following modifications that we made to the BookPubApplication class:

- ▸ The @SpringBootApplication annotation was replaced with three alternative annotations: @Configuration, @EnableAutoConfiguration, and @ComponentScan(excludeFilters=@ComponentScan. Filter(UsedForTesting.class)). The reason we had to do this was that we can add the excludeFilters attributes to the @ComponentScan annotation. Otherwise, the @SpringBootApplication meta/convenience annotation internally declared the exact three annotations; we just unrolled them as the explicit annotations of our application class. In our explicit declaration of the @ComponentScan annotation, we told Spring to ignore any configuration classes that have been annotated with an @UsedForTesting annotation.

- ▸ The @UsedForTesting annotation is what we added as an additional outer declaration to the BookPubApplication class. We used it in order to annotate our TestMockBeansConfig class, thus letting Spring know not to include it when the application is being booted in a regular, nontest mode.

With the application changes examined, let's now look at what we did in the TestMockBeansConfig configuration class:

- ▸ The @Configuration annotation tells Spring that this class contains the Application Context configuration and @Bean declarations and if included, these should be added to the created context.

- ▸ The @UsedForTesting annotation marks this class as test-only. We discussed this earlier.

- ▸ The @Primary annotation on the createMockPublisherRepository() method is how we will tell Spring to prefer this instance of the bean during an autowiring selection if multiple instances of the class are available. In our application, we already have the PublisherRepository instance created during the application startup because we have this interface annotated with @RepositoryRestResource. Thus, Spring already knows that it has to create an instance of this class and add it to the context. As we don't want to use the real instance for our test but prefer to use the Mockito mocked one, using the @Primary annotation allows us to accomplish exactly this.

Now that we know how the mocked instance of `PublisherRepository` gets injected into our tests, let's take a look at the newly created test class itself. The two methods of particular interest are `setupPublisherRepositoryMock()` and `resetPublisherRepositoryMock()`. They are described as follows:

▸ The `setupPublisherRepositoryMock()` method is annotated with `@Before`, which tells JUnit to execute this method before running every `@Test` method in the class. In this, we will use the Mockito framework in order to configure the behavior of our mocked instance. We will tell it that when `repository.count()` method is called, return `1` as a result. The Mockito library provides us with many convenient DLS-like methods, which we can use to define such rules with an English-like, easy-to-read style.

▸ The `resetPublisherRepositoryMock()` method is annotated with `@After`, which tells JUnit to execute this method after running every `@Test` method in the class. At the end of every test, we will need to reset the mocked behavior, so we will use the `Mockito.reset(...)` method call to clear out all of our settings and get the Mock ready for the next test, which can be used from another test suite altogether.

Writing tests using Cucumber

Unit testing has been an expected part of the software development lifecycle for quite some time now and one can hardly imagine writing code without having unit tests along with it. The art of testing does not stay the same and the advances in the testing philosophies have extended the concept of unit testing even further, introducing things such as service testing, integration testing, and lastly, what is known as **Behavior Driven Development**. Behavior Driven Development proposes to create the test suites describing the application behavior at large, and not getting down too much to the minute implementation details at the lower levels of the code. One such framework, which has gained a lot of popularity first in the Ruby world and later expanding to other languages including Java, is the Cucumber BDD.

For the purpose of this recipe, we will pick up from our previous example and continue enhancing the testing suite by adding the Cucumber-JVM implementation, which will provide us with the Java-based version of the original Ruby Cucumber framework and create a few tests in order to demonstrate the capabilities and integration points with the Spring Boot application.

 This recipe is by no means intended to cover the entire set of functionalities provided by the Cucumber testing framework and is mostly focused on the integration points of Cucumber and Spring Boot. To learn more about Cucumber-JVM, you can go to `https://cukes.info/docs#cucumber-implementations` or `https://github.com/cucumber/cucumber-jvm` for details.

How to do it...

1. The first thing that we need to do is add the necessary dependencies for the Cucumber libraries to our `build.gradle` file, as follows:

```
dependencies {
    compile("org.springframework.boot:spring-boot-starter-data-
            jpa")
    compile("org.springframework.boot:spring-boot-starter-jdbc")
    compile("org.springframework.boot:spring-boot-starter-web")
    compile("org.springframework.boot:spring-boot-starter-data-
            rest")
    compile project(':db-count-starter')
    runtime("com.h2database:h2")
    runtime("mysql:mysql-connector-java")
    testCompile("org.springframework.boot:spring-boot-starter-
                test")
    testCompile("info.cukes:cucumber-spring:1.2.2")
    testCompile("info.cukes:cucumber-java8:1.2.2")
    testCompile("info.cukes:cucumber-junit:1.2.2")
    testRuntime("com.jayway.jsonpath:json-path")
}
```

2. Next, we will need to create a test driver class to run Cucumber tests. Let's create a `RunCukeTests.java` file in the `src/test/java/org/test/bookpub` directory at the root of our project with the following content:

```
@RunWith(Cucumber.class)
@CucumberOptions(plugin={"pretty", "html:build/reports/cucumber"},
                glue = {"cucumber.api.spring",
                        "classpath:org.test.bookpub"},
                monochrome = true)
public class RunCukeTests {
}
```

3. With the driver class created, we are ready to start writing what Cucumber refers to as **Step Definitions**. I will talk briefly about what these are in the *How it works...* section of this recipe For now, let's create a `RepositoryStepdefs.java` file in the `src/test/java/org/test/bookpub` directory at the root of our project with the following content:

```
@WebAppConfiguration
@ContextConfiguration(classes = {BookPubApplication.class,
  TestMockBeansConfig.class}, loader =
    SpringApplicationContextLoader.class)
public class RepositoryStepdefs {
    @Autowired
```

```
    private WebApplicationContext context;
    @Autowired
    private DataSource ds;
    @Autowired
    private BookRepository bookRepository;

    private Book loadedBook;

    @Given("^([^\\\"]*) fixture is loaded$")
    public void data_fixture_is_loaded(String fixtureName) throws
Throwable {
        ResourceDatabasePopulator populator = new ResourceData
basePopulator(context.getResource("classpath:/" + fixtureName +
".sql"));
        DatabasePopulatorUtils.execute(populator, ds);
    }


    @Given("^(\\d+) books available in the catalogue$")
    public void books_available_in_the_catalogue(int bookCount)
throws Throwable {
        assertEquals(bookCount, bookRepository.count());
    }


    @When("^searching for book by isbn ([\\d-]+)$")
    public void searching_for_book_by_isbn(String isbn) throws
Throwable {
        loadedBook = bookRepository.findBookByIsbn(isbn);
        assertNotNull(loadedBook);
        assertEquals(isbn, loadedBook.getIsbn());
    }


    @Then("^book title will be ([^\"]*)$")
    public void book_title_will_be(String bookTitle) throws
Throwable {
        assertNotNull(loadedBook);
        assertEquals(bookTitle, loadedBook.getTitle());
    }
}
```

4. Now, we will need to create a corresponding testing feature definition file named `repositories.feature` in the `src/test/resources/org/test/bookpub` directory at the root of our project with the following content:

```
@txn
Feature: Finding a book by ISBN
  Background: Preload DB Mock Data
    Given packt-books fixture is loaded

  Scenario: Load one book
    Given 3 books available in the catalogue
    When searching for book by isbn 978-1-78398-478-7
    Then book title will be Orchestrating Docker
```

5. Lastly, we will create one more data SQL file named `packt-books.sql` in the `src/test/resources` directory at the root of our project with the following content:

```
INSERT INTO author (id, first_name, last_name) VALUES (5,
'Shrikrishna', 'Holla')
INSERT INTO book (isbn, title, author_id, publisher_id) VALUES
('978-1-78398-478-7', 'Orchestrating Docker', 5, 1)
```

6. Execute the tests by running `./gradlew clean test` and the tests should get passed.

7. With the addition of Cucumber, we also get the results of the tests in both the JUnit report and Cucumber-specific report HTML files. If we open `build/reports/tests/index.html` in the browser and click the **Classes** button, we will see our scenario in the table, as shown in the following screenshot:

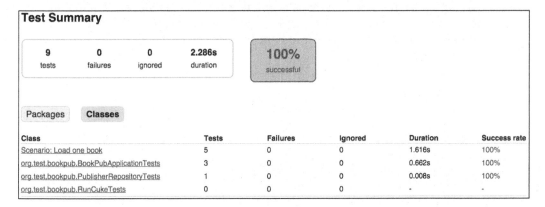

Class	Tests	Failures	Ignored	Duration	Success rate
Scenario: Load one book	5	0	0	1.616s	100%
org.test.bookpub.BookPubApplicationTests	3	0	0	0.662s	100%
org.test.bookpub.PublisherRepositoryTests	1	0	0	0.008s	100%
org.test.bookpub.RunCukeTests	0	0	0	-	-

8. Selecting the **Scenario: Load one book** link will take us to the detailed report page, as shown:

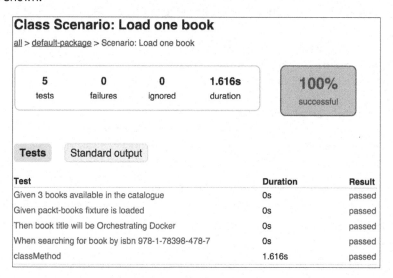

9. As we can see, the descriptions are nicer than the class and method names that we saw in the original JUnit-based test cases.

10. Cucumber also generates its own report, which can be viewed by opening `build/reports/cucumber/index.html` in the browser.

11. Being a behavior-driven testing framework, the feature files allow us to define not only individual conditions, but also declare entire scenario outlines, which make the defining of multiple assertions of similar data easier. Let's create another feature file named `restful.feature` in the `src/test/resources/org/test/bookpub` directory at the root of our project with the following content:

```
@txn
Feature: Finding a book via REST API
  Background:
    Given packt-books fixture is loaded

  Scenario Outline: Using RESTful API to lookup books by ISBN
    Given catalogue with books
    When requesting url /books/<isbn>
    Then status code will be 200
    And response content contains <title>

    Examples:
      |isbn            |title              |
      |978-1-78398-478-7|Orchestrating Docker|
      |978-1-78528-415-1|Spring Boot Recipes |
```

12. We will also create a corresponding `RestfulStepdefs.java` file in the `src/test/java/org/test/bookpub` directory at the root of our project with the following content:

```java
import cucumber.api.java.Before;
import cucumber.api.java.en.Given;
import cucumber.api.java.en.Then;
import cucumber.api.java.en.When;

import static org.hamcrest.CoreMatchers.containsString;
import static org.junit.Assert.assertTrue;
import static org.springframework.test.web.servlet.request.
MockMvcRequestBuilders.get;
import static org.springframework.test.web.servlet.result.
MockMvcResultMatchers.status;
import static org.springframework.test.web.servlet.result.
MockMvcResultMatchers.content;

@WebAppConfiguration
@ContextConfiguration(classes = {BookPubApplication.class,
  TestMockBeansConfig.class}, loader =
    SpringApplicationContextLoader.class)
public class RestfulStepdefs {
  @Autowired
  private WebApplicationContext context;
  @Autowired
  private BookRepository bookRepository;

  private MockMvc mockMvc;
  private ResultActions result;

  @Before
  public void setup() throws IOException {
    mockMvc =
      MockMvcBuilders.webAppContextSetup(context).build();
  }

  @Given("^catalogue with books$")
  public void catalogue_with_books() {
    assertTrue(bookRepository.count() > 0);
  }

  @When("^requesting url ([^\"]*)$")
  public void requesting_url(String url) throws Exception {
    result = mockMvc.perform(get(url));
  }
```

```
@Then("^status code will be ([\\d]*)$")
public void status_code_will_be(int code) throws
  Throwable {
  result.andExpect(status().is(code));
}

@Then("^response content contains ([^\"]*)$")
public void response_content_contains(String content)
  throws Throwable {
  result.andExpect(content().string(containsString(content)));
}
}
```

13. Execute the tests by running `./gradlew clean test` and the tests should continue to get passed.

How it works...

If you feel a bit lost after looking at all this code and following along without having a full understanding of what exactly is going on, here you will find the detailed breakdown of everything that we did.

Let's start with a quick overview of what Step Definitions are. As the Cucumber framework uses the Gherkin feature document files in order to describe the business rules that are to be tested, which are represented in a form of English-like sentence statements, these need to be translated into an executable code. This is the job of the Step Definition classes. Every step in a defined feature scenario needs to be matched to a method in a Step Definition class that will execute it. This matching is done by declaring a regular expression in the step annotations, such as @Given, @When, or @Then, placed above the methods. The regex contains the matching groups that Cucumber uses so as to extract the method arguments and pass them to the executing method.

In `RepositoryStepdefs`, we can see this in the following method:

```
@Given("^([^\\\"]*) fixture is loaded$")
public void data_fixture_is_loaded(String fixtureName) {...}
```

The `@Given` annotation contains the regex that matches the `Given packt-books fixture is loaded` line from `repositories.feature` and extracts the `packt-books` text from the pattern, which is then passed as a `fixtureName` argument to the method. The `@When` and `@Then` annotations work on exactly the same principle. So, in effect, what the Cucumber framework does is it matches the English-like worded rules from the feature files to the matched patterns of the executing methods and extracts parts of the rules as arguments to the matched methods.

> More information on Gherkin and how to use it can be found at `https://cukes.info/docs/reference#gherkin`.

With the basic Cucumber overview explained, let's shift our focus on how the tests integrate with Spring Boot and are configured.

It all starts with the driver harness class, which in our case is `RunCukeTests`. This class itself does not contain any tests but has two important annotations that stitch things together: `@RunWith(Cucumber.class)` and `@CucumberOptions`.

- ► `@RunWith(Cucumber.class)`: This is a JUnit annotation that indicates that the JUnit runner should use the Cucumber Feature files to execute the tests.
- ► `@CucumberOptions`: This provides an additional configuration for Cucumber.
    - ❑ `plugin={"pretty", "html:build/reports/cucumber"}`: This tells Cucumber to generate its reports in an html format in the `build/reports/cucumber` directory.
    - ❑ `glue = {"cucumber.api.spring", "classpath:org.test.bookpub"}`: This is a **VERY** important setting as it tells Cucumber which packages to load and from where to load them during the execution of the tests. The `cucumber.api.spring` package needs to be present in order to take advantage of the cucumber-spring integration library and the `org.test.bookpub` package is the location of our Step Definition implementation classes.
    - ❑ `monochrome = true`: This tells Cucumber not to print the output with the ANSI color as we integrate with JUnit and it will not look correct in the saved console output files.

> A complete list of the options can be found at `https://cukes.info/docs/reference/jvm#list-all-options`.

Now let's look at the `RepositoryStepdefs` class. It starts with the following annotations at the class level:

- ▸ `@WebAppConfiguration` tells Spring that this class needs `WebApplicationContext` initialized and it will be used for testing purposes during the execution

- ▸ `@ContextConfiguration(classes = {BookPubApplication. class, TestMockBeansConfig.class}, loader = SpringApplicationContextLoader.class)` instruct Spring to use the `BookPubApplication` and `TestMockBeansConfig` classes as a configuration for the Spring application context as well as to use the `SpringApplicationContextLoader` class from Spring Boot in order to bootstrap the testing harness

As the Cucumber-Spring integration does not know about Spring Boot, but only knows about Spring, we can't use the `@SpringApplicationConfiguration` meta-annotation. We have to resort to using only the annotations available from Spring proper, in order to stitch things together. Thankfully, we don't have to jump through many hoops, we just declare the exact annotation that `SpringApplicationConfiguration` encapsulates, by passing the desired configuration classes and loader to `@ContextConfiguration`.

Once the proper annotations are in place, Spring and Spring Boot will take over and provide us with the same convenience of autowiring beans as dependencies of our Step Definition classes.

One interesting characteristic of the Cucumber tests is the instantiation of a new instance of the Step Definition class for every execution of a scenario. Even though the method namespace is global—meaning that we can use the methods that are declared in the different Step Definition classes—they operate on states defined in them and are not shared. As a new instance gets created per scenario, the definition classes are stateful and rely on internal variables to keep a state among transitions from assertion to assertion. For example, in the `@When` annotated method, a particular state gets set and in the `@Then` annotated method, a set of assertions on that state gets evaluated. In our example of the `RepositoryStepdefs` class, we will internally set the state of the `loadedBook` class variable in its `searching_ for_book_by_isbn(...)` method, which later gets used to assert on so as to verify the match of the book's title in the `book_title_will_be` method afterwards. Due to this, if we mix the rules from the different definition classes in our feature files, the internal states would not be accessible among the multiple classes.

With the integration with Spring, this problem can be solved using the injection of the mocked objects—as we have seen in `PublisherRepositoryTests` from one of our previous examples—and have the shared `@Given` annotated method be used to set up the particular behavior of the mock for the given test. Then we can use the same dependency instance and inject it into another definition class that can be used in order to evaluate the `@Then` annotated assertion methods.

Another approach is the one that we saw in the second definition class, `RestfulStepdefs`, where we injected the `BookRepository`. However, in `restful.feature`, we will be using the `Given packt-books fixture is loaded` directive that translates to the invocation of `data_fixture_is_loaded` method from the `RepositoryStepdefs` class, which shares the same instance of the injected `BookRepository` object, inserting `packt-books.sql` data into it.

Another neat feature of the Cucumber and Spring integration is the use of the `@txn` annotation in the feature files. This tells Spring to execute the tests in a transaction wrapper, reset the database between the test executions, and guarantee a clean database state for every test.

Due to the global method namespace among all the Step Definition classes and test behavior defining feature files, we can use the power of the Spring injection to our advantage so as to reuse the testing models and have a common setup logic for all of the tests, thus making the tests behave similarly to how our application would function in the real production environment.

Writing tests using Spock

Another, no less popular, testing framework is Spock, which is written in Groovy by Peter Niederwieser. Being a Groovy-based framework, it is ideally suited to create testing suites for a majority of the JVM-based languages, especially for Java and Groovy itself. The dynamic language traits of Groovy make it well suited to write elegant, efficient, and expressive specifications in the Groovy language itself without the need for translations, as it is done in Cucumber with the help of the Gherkin library. As Spock is based on top of JUnit, integrating with it through JUnit's `@RunWith` facility, just like Cucumber does, is an easy enhancement to the traditional unit tests. It works well with all the existing tools, which have built-in support or integration with JUnit.

In this recipe, we will pick up from the previous recipe and enhance our test collection with a couple of Spock-based tests. In these tests, we will see how to set up MockMVC using the Spring dependency injection and testing harnesses. These will be used by the Spock test specifications in order to validate the fact that our data repository services will return the data as expected.

How to do it...

1. In order to add the Spock tests to our application, we will need to make a few changes to our `build.gradle` file first. As Spock tests are written in Groovy, the first thing to do is add a groovy plugin to our `build.gradle` file, as follows:

```
apply plugin: 'java'
apply plugin: 'groovy'
apply plugin: 'eclipse'
apply plugin: 'idea'
apply plugin: 'spring-boot'
```

2. We will also need to add the necessary Spock framework dependencies to the `build.gradle` dependencies block:

```
dependencies {
   ...
   testCompile('org.spockframework:spock-core:1.0-groovy-2.4')
   testCompile('org.spockframework:spock-spring:1.0-groovy-2.4')
   ...
}
```

3. As the tests will be in Groovy, we will need to create a new source directory for the files. Let's create the `src/test/groovy/org/test/bookpub` directory in the root of our project.

4. Now we are ready to write our first test. Create a `SpockBookRepositorySpecification.groovy` file in the `src/test/groovy/org/test/bookpub` directory at the root of our project with the following content:

```
@WebAppConfiguration
@ContextConfiguration(
   classes = [BookPubApplication.class,
     TestMockBeansConfig.class], loader =
       SpringApplicationContextLoader.class)
class SpockBookRepositorySpecification extends Specification {
   @Autowired
   private ConfigurableWebApplicationContext context

   @Shared
   boolean sharedSetupDone = false

   @Autowired
   private DataSource ds;

   @Autowired
   private BookRepository repository;
```

```
@Shared
private MockMvc mockMvc;

void setup() {
  if (!sharedSetupDone) {
    mockMvc =
      MockMvcBuilders.webAppContextSetup(context).build();

    sharedSetupDone = true
  }
  ResourceDatabasePopulator populator =
    new ResourceDatabasePopulator(
      context.getResource("classpath:/packt-books.sql"));
  DatabasePopulatorUtils.execute(populator, ds);
}

@Transactional
def "Test RESTful GET"() {
  when:
    def result = mockMvc.perform(get("/books/${isbn}"));

  then:
    result.andExpect(status().isOk())
    result.andExpect(content().string(containsString(title)));

  where:
    isbn              | title
  "978-1-78398-478-7"|"Orchestrating Docker"
  "978-1-78528-415-1"|"Spring Boot Recipes"
}

@Transactional
def "Insert another book"() {
  setup:
  def existingBook = repository.findBookByIsbn("978-1-
    78528-415-1")
  def newBook = new Book("978-1-12345-678-9",
    "Some Future Book", existingBook.getAuthor(),
      existingBook.getPublisher())
```

```
    expect:
    repository.count() == 3

    when:
      def savedBook = repository.save(newBook)

    then:
      repository.count() == 4
      savedBook.id > -1
  }
}
```

5. Execute the tests by running `./gradlew clean test` and the tests should get passed.

6. As Spock integrates with JUnit, we can see the execution report of the Spock tests together with the rest of our test suite. If we open `build/reports/tests/index.html` in the browser and click the **Classes** button, we will see our specification in the table, as shown in the following screenshot:

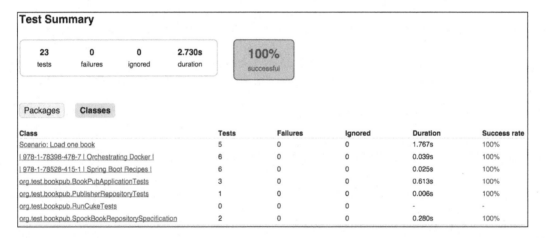

Test Summary

23	0	0	2.730s	100%
tests	failures	ignored	duration	successful

Packages **Classes**

Class	Tests	Failures	Ignored	Duration	Success rate
Scenario: Load one book	5	0	0	1.767s	100%
	978-1-78398-478-7	Orchestrating Docker		6	0	0	0.039s	100%
	978-1-78528-415-1	Spring Boot Recipes		6	0	0	0.025s	100%
org.test.bookpub.BookPubApplicationTests	3	0	0	0.613s	100%
org.test.bookpub.PublisherRepositoryTests	1	0	0	0.006s	100%
org.test.bookpub.RunCukeTests	0	0	0	-	-
org.test.bookpub.SpockBookRepositorySpecification	2	0	0	0.280s	100%

7. Selecting the **org.test.bookpub.SpockBookRespositorySpecification** link will take us to the detailed report page, which is as follows:

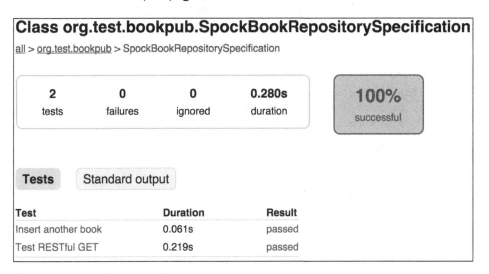

Class org.test.bookpub.SpockBookRepositorySpecification

all > org.test.bookpub > SpockBookRepositorySpecification

2	0	0	0.280s	100%
tests	failures	ignored	duration	successful

Tests   Standard output

Test	Duration	Result
Insert another book	0.061s	passed
Test RESTful GET	0.219s	passed

8. Next, we will take our tests a bit further and explore the mocking functionality of the database repositories. Let's use the existing `PublisherRepository`—for which we have already created a Mockito object mock in `TestMockBeansConfig`—and wire it into the `BookController` class to provide a `getBooksByPublisher` functionality. Let's add the following content to the `BookController` class in the `src/main/java/org/test/bookpub/controllers` directory at the root of our project:

```
@Autowired
private PublisherRepository publisherRepository;

@RequestMapping(value = "/publisher/{id}", method = RequestMethod.
GET)
public List<Book> getBooksByPublisher(@PathVariable("id") Long id)
{
    Publisher publisher = publisherRepository.findOne(id);
    Assert.notNull(publisher);
    return publisher.getBooks();
}
```

9. We will also need to add another annotation to our `Book` and `Publisher` entity classes. Let's add the following to the `Book` and `Publisher` classes in the `src/main/java/org/test/bookpub/entity` directory at the root of our project:

```
@JsonIdentityInfo(generator=ObjectIdGenerators.PropertyGenerator.
class, property="id", scope=Book.class)
public class Book {...}


@JsonIdentityInfo(generator=ObjectIdGenerators.PropertyGenerator.
class, property="id", scope=Publisher.class)
public class Publisher {...}
```

10. Lastly, let's add a getter and setter for the books to the `Publisher` entity class as well:

```
public List<Book> getBooks() {
    return books;
}


public void setBooks(List<Book> books) {
    this.books = books;
}
```

11. With all the code additions completed, we are ready to add another test to the `SpockBookRepositorySpecification.groovy` file in the `src/test/groovy/org/test/bookpub` directory at the root of our project with the following content:

```
...
class SpockBookRepositorySpecification extends Specification {
    ...
    @Autowired
    private PublisherRepository publisherRepository

    def "Test RESTful GET books by publisher"() {
        setup:
        Publisher publisher =
          new Publisher("Strange Books")
        publisher.setId(999)
        Book book = new Book("978-1-98765-432-1",
                "Mystery Book",
                new Author("John", "Doe"),
                publisher)
        publisher.setBooks([book])
        Mockito.when(publisherRepository.count()).
                thenReturn(1L)
        Mockito.when(publisherRepository.findOne(1L)).
```

```
                        thenReturn(publisher)

            when:
            def result =
              mockMvc.perform(get("/books/publisher/1"))

            then:
            result.andExpect(status().isOk())
            result.andExpect(content().
                    string(containsString("Strange Books")))

            cleanup:
            Mockito.reset(publisherRepository)
        }
    }
```

12. Execute the tests by running `./gradlew clean test` and the tests should continue to get passed.

How it works...

As you saw from this example, writing tests can be just as elaborate and sophisticated as the production code being tested itself. Let's examine the steps that we took in order to get the Spock tests integrated in our Spring Boot application.

The first thing that we did was to add a `groovy` plugin in order to make our build Groovy-friendly and we also added the required Spock library dependencies of `spock-core` and `spock-spring`, both of which are required to make Spock work with Spring's dependency injection and contexts.

The next step was to create the `SpockBookRepositorySpecification` Spock specification, which extends the Spock's `Specification` abstract base class. Extending the `Specification` class is very important because this is how JUnit knows that our class is the test class that needs to be executed. If we look in the `Specification` source, we will see the `@RunWith(Sputnik.class)` annotation, similar to the one that we used in the Cucumber recipe. In addition to the JUnit bootstrapping, the `Specification` class provides us with many helpful methods and mocking support as well.

 For more information about the detailed capabilities that are offered by Spock, you can refer to the Spock documentation that is available at `http://spockframework.github.io/spock/docs/1.0/index.html`.

It is also worth mentioning that we used the same annotations for the
SpockBookRepositorySpecification class as we did for our Cucumber-based tests, as
shown in the following code:

```
@WebAppConfiguration
@ContextConfiguration(
        classes = [BookPubApplication.class,
                   TestMockBeansConfig.class],
        loader = SpringApplicationContextLoader.class)
```

The reason that we had to resort to using these instead of just using
@SpringApplicationConfiguration is exactly the same as well. Neither the Spock
nor the Cucumber frameworks know about Spring Boot explicitly and thus are not capable
of recognizing its meta/convenience annotations. The good news is that we can always use
the same annotations as they are just regular Spring ones and annotate our classes directly,
which is exactly what we did.

Unlike Cucumber, Spock combines all the aspects of the test in one Specification class,
dividing it into multiple blocks, as follows:

▶ setup: This block is used to configure the specific test with variables, populating
  data, building mocks, and so on.

▶ expect: This block is one of the stimulus blocks, as Spock defines it, designed to
  contain simple expressions asserting a state or condition. Besides evaluating the
  conditions, we can only define variables in this block and nothing else is allowed.

▶ when: This block is another stimulus type block, which always goes together with
  then. It can contain any arbitrary code and is designed to define the behavior that
  we are trying to test.

▶ then: This block is a response type block. It is similar to expect: and can only
  contain conditions, exception checking, variable definition, and object interactions,
  such as how many times a particular method has been called and so forth.

 More information on interaction testing is available on Spock's website
at http://spockframework.github.io/spock/docs/1.0/
interaction_based_testing.html.

▶ cleanup: This block is used to clean the state of the environment and potentially
  undo whatever changes were done as part of the individual test execution. In our
  recipe, this is where we will reset our publisherRepository mock object.

Spock provides us with the instance-based setup() and cleanup() methods as well,
which can be used to define the setup and cleanup behavior that is common to all the
tests in the specification.

If we look at our `setup()` method, this is where we can configure the database population with the test data and build the MockMvc object. An interesting and important nuance is the use of the `sharedSetupDone` variable. In Spock, any field that is annotated with an `@Shared` annotation means that the same object will be used for all the tests. The problem is that Spring cannot inject the static fields with data, only the per-instance ones. So, we will use the `sharedSetupDone` field to track if we already ran the `setup()` method and created the `mockMvc` field, and so we don't end up starting a new container for the execution of every single test, thus saving a significant amount of time during the test execution.

Another helpful annotation is the `@Transactional` annotation of the test methods. Just as with the `@txn` tag in the Cucumber feature files, this annotation instructs Spock to execute the annotated method and its corresponding `setup()` and `cleanup()` executions with a transaction scope, which gets rolled back after the particular test method is finished. We rely on this behavior to get a clean database state for every test so that we don't end up inserting duplicate data during the execution of the `setup()` method every time each of our tests runs.

Most of you are probably wondering why we had to add the `@JsonIdentityInfo( generator=ObjectIdGenerators.PropertyGenerator.class, property="id")` annotation to our `Book` and `Publisher` entity classes. The answer has to do with the Jackson JSON parser and how it handles circular dependency. In our model, we have a Book belonging to a Publisher and each Publisher having multiple Books. When we created our `Publisher` with the `Books` mock and assigned a publisher instance to a book—which later got put in the publisher's book collection—we created a circular reference. During the execution of the `BookController.getBooksByPublisher(...)` method, the Jackson renderer would have thrown `StackOverflowError` while trying to write the object model to JSON. By adding this annotation to the `Book` and `Publisher` classes, we told Jackson to use the reference identifier instead of trying to write out the complete object, thus avoiding the circular reference loop situation.

The last thing that is important to keep in mind is how Spring Boot handles and processes the repository interfaces that are annotated with `@RepositoryRestResource`. Unlike the `BookRepository` interface, which we have annotated with a plain `@Repository` annotation and later explicitly declared as an autowire dependency of our `BookController` class, we did not create an explicit controller to handle RESTful requests for the rest of our repository interfaces such as the `PublisherRepository` and others. These interfaces get scanned by Spring Boot and automatically wrapped with the mapped endpoints that trap the requests and delegate the calls to the backing `SimpleJpaRepository` proxy. Due to this setup, we can use only the `@Primary` mock object replacement approach for these objects that have been explicitly injected as bean dependencies such as with our example of `BookRepository`. The good news is that in these situations, where we don't explicitly expect beans to be wired and only use some annotations to stereotype the interfaces for Spring Boot to do its magic, we can rely on Spring Boot to do the job correctly and know that it has tested all the functionalities behind it so that we don't have to test them.

6

Application Packaging and Deployment

In this chapter, we will cover the following topics:

- ▶ Creating a Spring Boot executable JAR
- ▶ Creating Docker images
- ▶ Building self-executing binaries
- ▶ Spring Boot environment configuration hierarchy and precedence
- ▶ Externalizing an environmental configuration using property files
- ▶ Externalizing an environmental configuration using environment variables
- ▶ Externalizing an environmental configuration using Java system properties
- ▶ Setting up Consul
- ▶ Externalizing an environmental configuration using Consul and envconsul

Introduction

What good is an application unless it is being used? In today's day and age—when DevOps became the way of doing software development, when Cloud is the king, and when building Microservices is considered as the thing to do—a lot of attention is being focused on how the applications get packaged, distributed, and deployed in their designated environments.

The Twelve-Factor App methodology has played an instrumental role in defining how a modern **Software as a Service** (**SaaS**) application is supposed to be built and deployed. One of the key principles is the separation of environmental configuration definitions from the application and storage of this in the environments. They also favor the isolation and bundling of the dependencies, development versus production parity, and ease of deployment and disposability of the applications, among others.

 The Twelve-Factor App methodology can be found at `http://12factor.net/`.

The DevOps model also encourages us to have complete ownership of our application, starting from writing and testing the code all the way to building and deploying it. If we are to assume this ownership, we need to ensure that the maintenance and overhead costs are not excessive and won't take away much time from our primary task of developing new features. This can be achieved by having clean, well-defined, and isolated deployable artifacts, which are self-contained, self-executed, and can be deployed in any environment without having to be rebuilt.

The following recipes will walk us through all the necessary steps to achieve the goals of low-effort deployment and maintenance while having a clean and elegant code behind it.

Creating a Spring Boot executable JAR

The Spring Boot magic would not be complete without providing a nice way to package the entire application including all of its dependencies, resources, and so on in one composite, executable JAR. After the JAR file is created, it can simply be launched by running a `java -jar <name>.jar` command.

We will continue with the application code that we built in the previous chapters and will add the necessary functionalities to package it. Let's go ahead and take a look at how to create the Spring Boot Uber JAR.

 The Uber JAR is typically known as an application bundle encapsulated in a single composite jar that internally contains a /lib directory with all the dependent inner jars and optionally a /bin directory with the executables.

How to do it...

1. Let's go to our code directory from *Chapter 5, Application Testing*, and execute `./gradlew clean build`.

2. With the Uber JAR built, let's launch the application by executing `java -jar build/libs/bookpub-0.0.1-SNAPSHOT.jar`.

3. This will result in our application running in the jar with the following console output:

```
  .   ____          _            __ _ _
 /\\ / ___'_ __ _ _(_)_ __  __ _ \ \ \ \
( ( )\___ | '_ | '_| | '_ \/ _` | \ \ \ \
 \\/  ___)| |_)| | | | | || (_| |  ) ) ) )
  '  |____| .__|_| |_|_| |_\__, | / / / /
 =========|_|==============|___/=/_/_/_/
 :: Spring Boot ::  (v1.3.0.BUILD-SNAPSHOT)

...

(The rest is omitted for conciseness)

...

2015-05-08 INFO: Registering beans for JMX exposure on startup

2015-05-08 INFO: Tomcat started on port(s): 8080 (http) 8443
(https)

2015-05-08 INFO: Welcome to the Book Catalog System!

2015-05-08 INFO: BookRepository has 1 entries

2015-05-08 INFO: ReviewerRepository has 0 entries

2015-05-08 INFO: PublisherRepository has 1 entries

2015-05-08 INFO: AuthorRepository has 1 entries

2015-05-08 INFO: Started BookPubApplication in 12.156 seconds (JVM
running for 12.877)

2015-05-08 INFO: Number of books: 1
```

How it works...

As you can see, getting the packaged executable JAR is fairly straightforward. All the magic is already coded and provided to us as part of the Spring Boot Gradle plugin. The addition of the plugin adds a number of tasks, which allow us to package the Spring Boot application together, run it, and build JAR, TAR, WAR files, and so on. For example, the `bootRun` task, which we have been using throughout this book, is provided by Spring Boot Gradle plugin, among others. We can see the complete list of the available Gradle tasks by executing `./gradlew tasks`. When we run this command, we will get the following output:

```
------------------------------------------------------------
All tasks runnable from root project
------------------------------------------------------------


Application tasks
```

----

bootRun - Run the project with support for auto-detecting main class and reloading static resources

installApp - Installs the project as a JVM application along with libs and OS specific scripts.

run - Runs this project as a JVM application

Build tasks

----

assemble - Assembles the outputs of this project.

bootRepackage - Repackage existing JAR and WAR archives so that they can be executed from the command line using 'java -jar'

build - Assembles and tests this project.

buildDependents - Assembles and tests this project and all projects that depend on it.

buildNeeded - Assembles and tests this project and all projects it depends on.

classes - Assembles classes 'main'.

clean - Deletes the build directory.

jar - Assembles a jar archive containing the main classes.

testClasses - Assembles classes 'test'.

Build Setup tasks

----

init - Initializes a new Gradle build. [incubating]

Distribution tasks

----

assembleMainDist - Assembles the main distributions

distTar - Bundles the project as a distribution.

distZip - Bundles the project as a distribution.

installDist - Installs the project as a distribution as-is.

The preceding output is not complete; I've excluded the non relevant task groups such as IDE, Documentation, and so on, but you will see them in your console. In the task list, we will see tasks such as bootRun, bootRepackage, and others. These tasks have been added by the Spring Boot Gradle plugin in order to enhance the build pipeline and produce the proper Spring Boot application bundle or start it. You can see the actual task dependency if you execute ./gradlew tasks --all, which will not only print the visible tasks, but also the depended, internal tasks and the task dependencies. For example, when we were running the build task, all the following depended tasks were executed as well:

build - Assembles and tests this project. [assemble, check]

assemble - Assembles the outputs of this project. [bootRepackage, distTar, distZip, jar]

You can see that the build task will execute the assemble task, which in turn, will call bootRepackage where the creation of the Uber JAR is actually taking place.

The plugin also provides a number of very useful configuration options. While I am not going to go into detail on all of them, I'll mention the two that I find very useful:

First configuration allows us to specify the executable JAR file classifier, creating a regular JAR containing just the application code and a separate executable JAR with the classifier in the name, bookpub-0.0.1-SNAPSHOT-exec.jar.

```
bootBoot {
  classifier = 'exec'
}
```

Another useful configuration option allows us to specify which dependency JARs require unpacking because, for some reason, they can't be included as nested inner JARs. This comes in very handy when you need something to be available in **System Classloader** such as setting a custom SecurityManager via the startup system properties:

```
springBoot {
  requiresUnpack = ['org.group.name:some-artifact']
}
```

In this example, the contents of the some-artifact JAR from the org.group dependency will be inlined in the main JAR along with the Spring Boot bootstrap code and the application code itself.

Creating Docker images

Docker, Docker, Docker! I hear this phrase more and more in all the conferences and tech meetups that I attend. The arrival of Docker has been welcomed by the community with open arms and it has instantly become a hit. The Docker ecosystem has been rapidly expanding with many other companies providing services, support, and complimenting frameworks such as Apache Mesos and Amazon Elastic Beanstalk, just to name a few. Even Microsoft has embraced the technology and is working on providing Docker support in their Azure Cloud service.

The reason for Docker's overwhelming popularity lies behind the ability that it provides to package and deploy applications in a form of self-contained containers. The containers are more lightweight than the traditional full-blown virtual machines. Multiple numbers of them can be run on top of a single OS instance, thus increasing the number of applications that can be deployed on the same hardware as compared to traditional VMs.

In this recipe, we will take a look at what it would take to package our Spring Boot application as a Docker image and how to deploy and run it.

Building a Docker image and just running it on your development machine is doable, but not as much fun as being able to share it with the world. You will need to publish it somewhere for it to be deployable, especially if you are thinking of doing it in Amazon or some other cloud-like environment. Luckily, Docker provides us with not only the Container solution, but also with a repository service, DockerHub, located at `https://hub.docker.com` where we can create repositories and publish our Docker images. So think of it like Maven Central for Docker.

How to do it...

1. The first step will be to create an account on DockerHub so that we can publish our images. Go to `https://hub.docker.com` and create an account. You can also use your GitHub account and log in using it if you have one.

2. Once you have an account, we will need to create a repository named `springbootcookbook`.

3. With this account created, now is the time to build the image. For this, we will use one of the Gradle Docker plugins. We will start by changing `build.gradle` to modify the buildscript block with the following change:

```
buildscript {
  dependencies {
    classpath("org.springframework.boot:spring-boot-gradle-
      plugin:${springBootVersion}")
    classpath("se.transmode.gradle:gradle-docker:1.2")
  }
}
```

4. We will also need to apply this plugin by adding the `apply plugin: 'docker'` directive to the `build.gradle` file.

5. Lastly, we will need to add the following Docker configuration to the `build.gradle` file as well:

```
distDocker {
  exposePort 8080
  exposePort 8443
  addFile
    file("${System.properties['user.home']}/.keystore"),
      "/root/"
}
```

6. Assuming that you already have Docker installed on your machine, we can proceed to create the image by executing `./gradlew clean distDocker`.

 For Docker installation instructions, please visit the tutorial that is located at `https://docs.docker.com/installation/#installation`.

7. If everything has worked out correctly, you should see the following output:

```
$ ./gradlew distDocker
...
:compileGroovy UP-TO-DATE
:processResources UP-TO-DATE
:classes UP-TO-DATE
:jar UP-TO-DATE
:findMainClass
:startScripts UP-TO-DATE
:distTar UP-TO-DATE
:distDocker
Sending build context to Docker daemon 30.46 MB
Sending build context to Docker daemon
Step 0 : FROM aglover/java8-pier
 ---> 69f4574a230e
Step 1 : EXPOSE 8080
 ---> Using cache
 ---> 725f1fd8c808
Step 2 : EXPOSE 8443
 ---> Using cache
```

```
---> d552630db9d5
Step 3 : ADD .keystore /root/
 ---> d0684cbd7fac
Removing intermediate container ef2dffe243f4
Step 4 : ADD ch6.tar /
 ---> a0963c837391
Removing intermediate container fb140e526e29
Step 5 : ENTRYPOINT /ch6/bin/ch6
 ---> Running in a769b6d6b40b
 ---> 778da2170839
Removing intermediate container a769b6d6b40b
Successfully built 778da2170839


BUILD SUCCESSFUL

Total time: 1 mins 0.009 secs
```

8. We can also execute `docker images` command to see the newly created image:

```
$ docker images
REPOSITORY            TAG              IMAGE ID
CREATED               VIRTUAL  SIZE
ch6                                    latest           778da2170839
17 minutes ago        1.04 GB
aglover/java8-pier    latest           69f4574a230e           11
months ago            1.01 GB
```

9. With the image built successfully, we are now ready to start it by executing the following command:

```
docker run -d -P ch6.
```

10. After the container has started, we can query the Docker registry for the port bindings so that we can access the HTTP endpoints for our service. This can be done by the `docker ps` command. If the container is running successfully, we should see the following result (names and ports will vary):

```
CONTAINER ID          IMAGE            COMMAND
CREATED               STATUS           PORTS
NAMES
```

```
37b37e411b9e          ch6:latest              "/ch6/bin/ch6"        10
minutes ago       Up 10 minutes        0.0.0.0:32778->8080/tcp,
0.0.0.0:32779->8443/tcp    drunk_carson
```

11. From this output, we can tell that the port mapping for the internal port `8080` has been set up to be `32778` (your port will vary for every run). Let's open `http://localhost:32778/books` in the browser to see our application in action, as shown in the following screenshot:

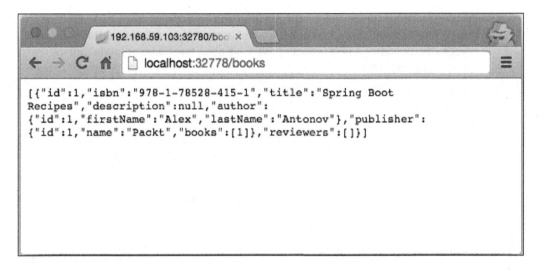

 If you are using a Mac OS X, you will be using boot2docker and thus won't be running the Docker container locally. In this scenario, you will be using `boot2docker ip` instead of the local host to connect to the application. For more good tips on how to make the boot2docker integration easier, please visit `http://viget.com/extend/how-to-use-docker-on-os-x-the-missing-guide`.

One can also use a nice Docker façade, generously created by Ian Sinnott, which would automatically start boot2docker and handle the environment variables as well. To get the wrapper, go to `https://gist.github.com/iansinnott/0a0c212260386bdbfafb`.

How it works...

In the preceding example, we have seen how easy it is to have our build package the application in a Docker container. The additional Gradle-Docker plugin does the bulk of the work of image building and publishing; all we have to do is give it some instructions on what and how we want the image to be. These are defined in the `distDocker` configuration block. Let's examine these instructions in detail:

- The `exposePort` directive tells the plugin to add an `EXPOSE <port>` instruction to the `Dockerfile` so that when our container is started, it will expose these internal ports to the outside via port mapping. We have seen this mapping while running the `docker ps` command.

- The `addFile` directive tells the plugin to add an `ADD <src> <dest>` instruction to the `Dockerfile` so that when the container is being built, we will copy the file from the source filesystem in the filesystem in the container image. In our case, we will need to copy the `.keystore` certificate file that we configured in one of our previous recipes for the HTTPS connector, which we instructed in `tomcat.https.properties` to be loaded from `${user.home}/.keystore`. Now, we need it to be in the `/root/` directory as, in the container, our application will be executed under root. (This can be changed with more configurations.)

 The Gradle-Docker plugin uses the project name as a name for the image by default. The project name, in turn, is being inferred by Gradle from the project's directory name, unless an explicit property value is configured. As in the code example for Chapter 6, the project directory is named `ch6`, thus the name of the image. The project name can be explicitly configured by adding `name='some_project_name'` in `gradle.properties`.

If you look at the resulting `Dockerfile`, which can be found in the `build/docker/` directory at the root of the project, you will see the following two instructions:

```
ADD ch6.tar /
ENTRYPOINT ["/ch6/bin/ch6"]
```

The `ADD` instruction adds the TAR application archive that was produced by the `distTar` task and contains our application bundled up as a tarball. We can even see the contents of the produced tarball by executing `tar tvf build/distributions/ch6.tar`. During the building of the container, the contents of the TAR file will be extracted in the `/` directory in the container and later used to launch the application.

It is followed by the `ENTRYPOINT` instruction. This tells Docker to execute `/ch6/bin/ch6`—which we saw to be a part of the tarball content—once the container is started, thus automatically launching our application.

The first line in the `Dockerfile`, which is `FROM aglover/java8-pier`, is the instruction to use the `aglover/java8-pier` image, which contains the Ubuntu OS with Java 8 installed, as a base image for our container, on which we will install our application. This image comes from the Docker Hub Repository and is automatically used by the plugin, but can be changed via the configuration settings, if so desired.

If you created an account on Docker Hub, we can also publish the created Docker image to the registry. In fair warning, the resulting image could be many hundreds of megabytes in size so uploading it could take some time. To publish this image, we will need to add the following two configuration settings to the `distDocker` configuration block in `build.gradle`:

```
distDocker {
    tag "<docker hub username>/<docker hub repository name>"
    push true
    exposePort 8080
    exposePort 8443
    addFile file("${System.properties['user.home']}/.keystore"),
        "/root/"
}
```

The `tag` property sets up the created image tag and by default, the plugin assumes that it is residing in the Docker Hub Repository; so this is where it will be publishing it if the `push` configuration is set to `true`, as it is in our case.

> For a complete list of all the Gradle-Docker plugin configuration options, take a look at the `https://github.com/Transmode/gradle-docker` Github project page.

When launching a Docker image, we used the `-d` and `-P` command-line arguments. Their uses are as follows:

- `-d`: This indicates the desire to run the container in a detached mode where the process starts in the background
- `-P`: This instructs Docker to publish all the internally exposed ports to the outside so that we can access them

> For a detailed explanation of all the possible command-line options, refer to `https://docs.docker.com/reference/commandline/cli/`.

Building self-executing binaries

Starting with Spring Boot version 1.3, the Gradle and Maven plugins support an option of generating true executable binaries, which look like normal JAR files, but have the content of JAR fused together with the launch script that contains the command-building logic and is capable of self-starting itself without the need to execute the `java -jar file.jar` command explicitly. This capability comes in very handy as it allows the easy configuration of the Linux autostart services such as `init.d` or `systemd` and `launchd` on OS X.

Getting ready

For this recipe, we will use our existing application build. We will examine how the self-starting executable JAR files get created and how to modify the default launch script to add support for the custom JVM start up arguments, such as the `-D` startup system properties, JVM memory, GC, and other settings.

For this recipe, make sure that `build.gradle` is using Spring Boot version 1.3 or above. If it is not, then change the following setting in the buildscript configuration block, as follows:

```
ext {
    springBootVersion = '1.3.0.BUILD-SNAPSHOT'
}
```

The same upgrade of the Spring Boot version should be done in the `db-counter-starter/build.gradle` file as well.

We need to explicitly add the `application` plugin to `build.gradle` as it is no longer automatically included by the Spring Boot Gradle plugin. Add `apply plugin: 'application'` to the list of plugins in the `build.gradle` file.

How to do it...

1. Building a default self-executing JAR file is very easy; actually it is done automatically once we execute the `./gradlew clean bootRepackage` command.

2. We can proceed to the launching of the created application simply by invoking `./build/libs/bookpub-0.0.1-SNAPSHOT.jar`.

3. For the enterprise environment, it is rare that we are satisfied with the default JVM launch arguments as we often need to tweak the memory settings, GC configurations, and even pass the start up system properties in order to ensure that we are using the desired version of the XML parser or a proprietary implementation of Class Loader or Security Manager. To accomplish this, we will modify the default `launch.script` file to add support for the JVM options. Let's start by copying the default `launch. script` file from the `https://github.com/spring-projects/spring-boot/ blob/master/spring-boot-tools/spring-boot-loader-tools/src/ main/resources/org/springframework/boot/loader/tools/launch. script` Spring Boot GitHub repository in the root of our project.

> The `launch.script` file is supported only on the Linux and OS X environments. If you are looking to make the self-executing JARs for Windows, you will need to provide your own `launch.script` file that is tailored for the Windows shell command execution. The good news is that it is the only special thing that is required; all the instructions and concepts in this recipe will work just fine on Windows as well, provided that the compliant `launch.script` template is being used.

4. We will modify the copied `launch.script` file and add the following content right above the line 90 mark: (This is showing only the relevant part of the script in order to condense the space usage.)

```
. . .
# Find Java
if [[ -n "$JAVA_HOME" ]] && [[ -x "$JAVA_HOME/bin/java" ]]; then
    javaexe="$JAVA_HOME/bin/java"
elif type -p java 2>&1> /dev/null; then
    javaexe=java
elif [[ -x "/usr/bin/java" ]];  then
    javaexe="/usr/bin/java"
else
    echo "Unable to find Java"
    exit 1
fi

# Configure JVM Options
jvmopts="{{jvm_options:}}"
if [[ -n "JAVA_OPTS" ]]; then
    jvmopts="$jvmopts $JAVA_OPTS"
fi
# Build actual command to execute
```

```
command="$javaexe $jvmopts -jar -Dsun.misc.URLClassPath.
disableJarChecking=true $jarfile $@"

# Action functions
start() {
...
```

5. With the custom `launch.script` file in place, we will need to add the options setting to our `build.gradle` file with the following content:

```
applicationDefaultJvmArgs = [
    "-Xms128m",
    "-Xmx256m"
]

springBoot {
    classifier = 'exec'
    embeddedLaunchScript = file('launch.script')
    embeddedLaunchScriptProperties = ['jvm_options' :
applicationDefaultJvmArgs.join(' ')]
}
```

6. We are now ready to launch our application. First, let's use the `./gradlew clean bootRun` command, and if we look at the JConsole VM Summary tab, we will see that our arguments indeed have been passed to the JVM, as follows:

Current heap size:	69,370 kbytes
Maximum heap size:	233,472 kbytes

Garbage collector:	Name = 'PS MarkSweep', Collections = 2, Total time spent = 0.136 seconds
Garbage collector:	Name = 'PS Scavenge', Collections = 34, Total time spent = 0.144 seconds

Operating System:	Mac OS X 10.10.3
Architecture:	x86_64
Number of processors:	8
Committed virtual memory:	4,299,488 kbytes

VM arguments:	-Xms128m -Xmx256m -Dfile.encoding=UTF-8 -Duser.country=US -Duser.language=en -Duser.variant

7. We can also build the self-starting executable JAR by running the `./gradlew clean bootRepackage` command and then executing `./build/libs/bookpub-0.0.1-SNAPSHOT-exec.jar` in order to launch our application and we should expect to see a similar result in JConsole.

8. Alternatively, we can also use the JAVA_OPTS environment variable to override some of the JVM arguments. Say we want to change the minimum memory heap size to 128 megabytes. We can launch our application using the JAVA_OPTS=-Xmx128m ./build/libs/bookpub-0.0.1-SNAPSHOT-exec.jar command and this would show us the following effect in JConsole:

Current heap size: 49,311 kbytes	**Committed memory:** 125,952 kbytes
Maximum heap size: 125,952 kbytes	**Pending finalization:** {0} objects
Garbage collector: Name = 'PS MarkSweep', Collections = 2, Total time spent = 0.207 seconds	
Garbage collector: Name = 'PS Scavenge', Collections = 81, Total time spent = 0.287 seconds	
Operating System: Mac OS X 10.10.3	**Total physical memory:** 16,777,216 kbytes
Architecture: x86_64	**Free physical memory:** 410,752 kbytes
Number of processors: 8	**Total swap space:** 5,242,880 kbytes
Committed virtual memory: 4,161,596 kbytes	**Free swap space:** 1,152,000 kbytes
VM arguments: -Xms128m -Xmx256m -Xmx128m -Dsun.misc.URLClassPath.disableJarChecking=true	

How it works...

With a small customization to launch.script, we were able to create a self-executing deployable application, packaged as a self-contained JAR file, which on top of all the things, can also be configured in order to be launched using the various OS-specific autostarting frameworks.

The Spring Boot Gradle and Maven plugins provide us with lots of options for parameter customization and even an ability to embed mustache-like template placeholders in launch.script, which can later be replaced with values during build time. We have leveraged this capability to inject our JVM arguments into the file using the embeddedLaunchScriptProperties configuration setting.

In our custom version of launch.script, we added the jvmopts="{{jvm_options:}}" line, which will be replaced with the value of the jvm_options parameter during the build and packaging time. This parameter is declared in our build.gradle file as a value of the embeddedLaunchScriptProperties argument: embeddedLaunchScriptProperties = ['jvm_options' : applicationDefaultJvmArgs.join(' ')].

The JVM arguments can be hardcoded, but it is much better to maintain the consistency between how our application starts using the bootRun task and how it starts when launched from the self-executing JAR. To achieve this, we will use the same applicationDefaultJvmArgs collection of arguments that we will define for the bootRun execution purpose, only with all the different arguments collapsed in a single line of text separated by white spaces. Using this approach, we have to define the JVM arguments only once and use them in both the modes of execution.

It is important to notice that this reuse also applies to the application distributions that are built using the distZip and distTar tasks defined by Gradle's application plugin.

We can modify the build to create the Docker image by launching our self-executing JAR instead of the contents of the TAR file produced by the distTar task by default. To do this, we will need to replace our distDocker configuration block with the following code:

```
task distDocker(type: Docker, overwrite: true, dependsOn:
  bootRepackage) {
  group = 'docker'
  description = "Packs the project's JVM application as a Docker
    image."
  inputs.files project.bootRepackage
  doFirst {
    tag "aantono/springbootcookbook"
    push false
    exposePort 8080
    exposePort 8443
    addFile file("${System.properties['user.home']}/.keystore"),
      "/root/"
    applicationName = project.applicationName
    addFile project.bootRepackage.outputs.files.singleFile

    def executableName = "/" +
      project.bootRepackage.outputs.files.singleFile.name
    entryPoint = ["$executableName"]
  }
}
```

This will effectively overwrite the existing distDocker task and replace it with ours.

Spring Boot environment config hierarchy and precedence

In the previous few recipes, we have seen how to package our application in a variety of ways and how it can be deployed. The next logical step is the need to configure the application in order to provide some behavioral control as well as some environment-specific configuration values, which could and most likely will vary from environment to environment.

A common example of such an environmental configuration difference is the database setup. We certainly don't want to connect to a production environment database with an application running on our development machine. There are also cases when we want an application to run in different modes or use a different set of profiles, as they are referred to by Spring. An example could be running an application in live or simulator mode.

For this recipe, we will pick up from the previous state of the codebase and add the support for different configuration profiles as well as examine how to use the property values as placeholders in other property definitions and how to add your own `PropertySource` implementation.

How to do it...

1. We will start by adding an `@Profile` annotation to the `@Bean` creation of `schedulerRunner` by changing the definition of the `schedulerRunner(...)` method in `BookPubApplication.java` located in the `src/main/java/org/test/bookpub` directory at the root of our project to the following content:

    ```
    @Bean
    @Profile("logger")
    public StartupRunner schedulerRunner() {
        return new StartupRunner();
    }
    ```

2. Start the application by running `./gradlew clean bootRun`.

3. Once the application is running, we should no longer see the previous log output from the `StartupRunner` class, which looked as follows:

    ```
    2015-05-29 --- org.test.bookpub.StartupRunner            : Number
    of books: 1
    ```

4. Now, let's build the application by running `./gradlew clean bootRepackage` and start it by running `./build/libs/bookpub-0.0.1-SNAPSHOT-exec.jar --spring.profiles.active=logger` and we will see the log output line showing up again.

5. Another functionality that is enabled by the **Profile** selector is the ability to add Profile-specific property files. Let's create an `application-inmemorydb.properties` file in the `src/main/resources` directory at the root of our project with the following content:

    ```
    spring.datasource.url = jdbc:h2:mem:testdb;DB_CLOSE_DELAY=-1;DB_
    CLOSE_ON_EXIT=FALSE
    ```

6. Let's build the application by running `./gradlew clean bootRepackage` and start it by running `./build/libs/bookpub-0.0.1-SNAPSHOT-exec.jar --spring.profiles.active=logger,inmemorydb`, which will use the `inmemorydb` Profile configuration in order to use the in-memory database instead of the file-based one.

In the cases where the enterprise is already using a particular configuration system, custom written or off the shelf, Spring Boot provides us with a facility to integrate this into the application via the creation of a custom `PropertySource` implementation.

Let's imagine that we have an existing configuration setup that uses a popular Apache Commons Configuration framework and stores the configuration data in XML files.

1. To mimic our supposed pre-existing configuration system, add the following content to the dependencies section in the `build.gradle` file:

```
dependencies {
    ...
    compile project(':db-count-starter')
    compile("commons-configuration:commons-configuration:1.10")
    compile("commons-codec:commons-codec:1.6")
    compile("commons-jxpath:commons-jxpath:1.3")
    compile("commons-collections:commons-collections:3.2.1")
    runtime("com.h2database:h2")
    ...
}
```

2. Follow this up by creating a simple configuration file named `commons-config.xml` in the `src/main/resources` directory at the root of our project with the following content:

```
<?xml version="1.0" encoding="ISO-8859-1" ?>
<config>
  <book>
    <counter>
      <delay>1000</delay>
      <rate>${book.counter.delay}0</rate>
    </counter>
  </book>
</config>
```

3. Next, we will create the `PropertySource` implementation file named `ApacheCommonsConfigurationPropertySource.java` in the `src/main/java/org/test/bookpub` directory at the root of our project with the following content:

```
public class ApacheCommonsConfigurationPropertySource
    extends EnumerablePropertySource<XMLConfiguration> {
    private static final Log logger = LogFactory.getLog(
    ApacheCommonsConfigurationPropertySource.class);

    public static final String
      COMMONS_CONFIG_PROPERTY_SOURCE_NAME = "commonsConfig";

    public ApacheCommonsConfigurationPropertySource(String name,
```

```
      XMLConfiguration source) {
        super(name, source);
    }

    @Override
    public String[] getPropertyNames() {
      ArrayList<String> keys =
        Lists.newArrayList(this.source.getKeys());
      return keys.toArray(new String[keys.size()]);
    }

    @Override
    public Object getProperty(String name) {
      return this.source.getString(name);
    }

    public static void addToEnvironment(
      ConfigurableEnvironment environment, XMLConfiguration
        xmlConfiguration) {
      environment.getPropertySources().addAfter(
        StandardEnvironment.
          SYSTEM_ENVIRONMENT_PROPERTY_SOURCE_NAME,
            new ApacheCommonsConfigurationPropertySource(
              COMMONS_CONFIG_PROPERTY_SOURCE_NAME,
                xmlConfiguration));
      logger.trace("ApacheCommonsConfigurationPropertySource
        add to Environment");
    }
  }
```

4. We will now create the `SpringApplicationRunListener`
    implementation class so as to bootstrap our `PropertySource` named
    `ApacheCommonsConfigurationApplicationRunListener.java` in the `src/
    main/java/org/test/bookpub` directory at the root of our project with the
    following content:

```
public class
  ApacheCommonsConfigurationApplicationRunListener
    implements SpringApplicationRunListener{

    public
      ApacheCommonsConfigurationApplicationRunListener(
        SpringApplication application, String[] args) {
    }

    @Override
```

```
public void started() {

}

@Override
public void environmentPrepared(
  ConfigurableEnvironment environment) {
    try {
      ApacheCommonsConfigurationPropertySource.
        addToEnvironment(environment,
          new XMLConfiguration("commons-config.xml"));
    }
    catch (ConfigurationException e) {
      throw new RuntimeException("Unable to load
        commons-config.xml", e);
    }
  }

@Override
public void
  contextPrepared(ConfigurableApplicationContext
    context) {

}

@Override
public void contextLoaded(ConfigurableApplicationContext
  context) {

}

@Override
public void finished(ConfigurableApplicationContext
  context, Throwable exception) {
  }
}
```

5. Finally, we will need to create a new directory named `META-INF` in the `src/main/resources` directory at the root of our project and create a file named `spring.factories` in it with the following content:

```
# Run Listeners
org.springframework.boot.SpringApplicationRunListener=\
org.test.bookpub.ApacheCommonsConfigurationApplicationRunListener
```

6. With all the setup done, we are now ready to use our new properties in our application. Let's change the configuration of the @Scheduled annotation for our StartupRunner class located in the src/main/java/org/test/bookpub directory at the root of our project, as follows:

    ```
    @Scheduled(initialDelayString = "${book.counter.delay}",
        fixedRateString = "${book.counter.rate}")
    ```

7. Let's build the application by running ./gradlew clean bootRepackage and start it by running ./build/libs/bookpub-0.0.1-SNAPSHOT-exec.jar --spring.profiles.active=logger in order to ensure that our StartupRunner class is still logging the book count every ten seconds, as expected.

How it works...

In this recipe, we experimented with the using of Profiles, applying additional configuration settings based on the active profiles, and adding our own custom PropertySource that allowed us to bridge the existing system in the Spring Boot environment. We will examine each of these in detail starting with the notion of Spring Profiles.

Profiles were first introduced in the Spring Framework 3.2 and used to conditionally configure the beans in context based on which profiles were active. In Spring Boot, this facility was extended even further to allow configuration separation as well.

By placing an @Profile("logger") annotation on our StartupRunner @Bean creation method, we told Spring to create the bean only if the logger profile has been activated. Conventionally, this is done by passing the --spring.profiles.active option in the command line during the application startup. In the tests, another way that this can be done is using the @ActiveProfiles("profile") annotation on the test class, but it is not supported for the execution of a normal application. It is also possible to negate profiles such as @Profile("!production"). When such an annotation is used (with ! marking the negation), the bean will be created only if no profile production is active.

During the startup, Spring Boot treats all the options that get passed via the command line as application properties, and thus anything that gets passed during the startup, ends up as a property value that is capable of being used. This same mechanism not only works for new properties but can be used as a way to override the already existing properties as well. Let's imagine a situation where we already have an active profile defined in our application.properties file that looks like this: spring.profiles.active=basic. By passing the --spring.profiles.active=logger option via the command line, we will replace the active profile from basic to logger. If we want to include some profiles regardless of the active configuration, Spring Boot gives us a spring.profiles.include option to configure. Any profiles that are set up this way will be added to the list of active profiles.

As these options are nothing more than regular Spring Boot application properties, they all follow the same hierarchy for override precedence. The options have been outlined as follows:

▶ **Command Line Arguments**: These values supersede every other property source in the list and you can always be rest assured that anything passed via `--property.name=value` will take precedence over the other means.

▶ **JNDI Attributes**: They are the next in seniority. If you are using an application container that provides data via a JNDI `java:comp/env` namespace, these values will override all the other settings from below.

▶ **Java System Properties**: These values are another way to pass the properties to the application either via the `-Dproperty=name` command line arguments or by calling `System.setProperty(...)` in the code. They provide another way to replace the existing properties. Anything coming from `System.getProperty(...)` will win over the others in the list below.

▶ **OS Environment Variables**: Either from Windows, Linux, OS X, or any other, they are a common way to specify a configuration, especially for locations and values. The most notable one is `JAVA_HOME`, which is a common way to indicate where the JVM location resides in the filesystem. If neither of the preceding settings are present, the `ENV` variables will be used for the property values instead of the ones mentioned as follows:

> As the OS Environment Variables typically don't support dots (`.`) or dashes (`-`), Spring Boot provides an automatic remapping mechanism that replaces the underscores (`_`) with dots (`.`) during the property evaluation as well as handles the case conversion. Thus, `JAVA_HOME` becomes synonymous to `java.home`.

▶ `random.*`: This provides a special support for the random values of primitive types that can be used as placeholders in configuration properties. For example, we can define a property named `some.number=${random.int}` where `${random.int}` will be replaced by some random integer value. The same goes for `${random.value}` for textual values and `${random.long}` for longs.

- ▸ `application-{profile}.properties`: These are the Profile-specific files that get applied only if a corresponding Profile gets activated.

- ▸ `application.properties`: These are the main property files that contain the base/default application configuration. Similar to the Profile-specific, these values can be loaded from the following list of locations, with the top one taking priority over the lower entries:
  - ❏ `file:config/`: This represents a `/config` directory located in the current directory
  - ❏ `file:`: This represents the current directory
  - ❏ `classpath:/config`: This represents a `/config` package in the classpath
  - ❏ `classpath:`: This represents a root of the classpath

- ▸ **@Configuration** annotated classes which are also annotated with **@PropertySource**: These are any in-code property sources that have been configured using annotations. We have seen an example of such a usage in our recipe from *Chapter 3, Web Framework Behavior Tuning* in the *Adding custom connectors* section. They are very low in the precedence chain and are only preceded by the default properties.

- ▸ **Default properties**: They are configured via the `SpringApplication.setDefaultProperties(...)` call and are seldom used, as it feels very much like hard coding values in code instead of externalizing them in configuration files.

Now that we know how the different configuration definitions stack up and which rules are used to overlay them on top of each other, let's look at the last part of our recipe: the bridging of Apache Commons Configuration using a custom `PropertySource` implementation. (This should not be confused with an `@PropertySource` annotation!)

In *Chapter 4, Writing Custom Spring Boot Starters* we learned about the use of `spring.factories`, and so we already know that this file serves to define the classes that should automatically be incorporated by Spring Boot during the application startup. The only difference this time is that instead of configuring the `EnableAutoConfiguration` settings, we will configure the `SpringApplicationRunListener` ones.

We created the following two classes to support our needs:

- ▶ ApacheCommonsConfigurationPropertySource: This is the extension of the EnumerablePropertySource base class that provides you with the internal functionality in order to bridge XMLConfiguration from Apache Commons Configuration to the world of Spring Boot by providing transformation to get the specific property values by name via the getProperty(String name) implementation and the list of all the supported property names via the getPropertyNames() implementation. In situations where you are dealing with the use case when the complete list of the available property names is not known or is very expensive to compute, we can just extend the PropertySource abstract class instead of using EnumerablePropertySource.

- ▶ ApacheCommonsConfigurationApplicationRunListener; This is the implementation of the SpringApplicationRunListener interface that gets instantiated by Spring Boot during the application startup and receives notification callbacks during the various stages of the application startup lifecycle. This class is configured in spring.factories and is automatically created by Spring Boot.

 It is *VERY* important to note that all the implementations of the SpringApplicationRunListener interface must define a public constructor with the exact signature of (SpringApplication application, String[] args) as this is what Spring Boot expects to be available when instantiating the class.

In our listener, we are interested in the environmentPrepared(ConfigurableEnvironment environment) callback, which gives us access to the ConfigurableEnvironment instance. By the time this callback is invoked, we will get an environment instance that has already been populated with all of the properties from the preceding hierarchy. However, we will get an opportunity to inject our own PropertySource implementation anywhere in the list, which we will successfully do in the ApacheCommonsConfigurationPropertySource.addToEnvironment(...) method.

In our case, we will choose to insert our source right below systemEnvironment in the order of precedence but if need be, we can alter this order to whatever highest precedence that we desire. Just be careful not to place it so high that your properties become impossible to override via the command-line arguments, system properties, or environment variables.

Externalizing environmental config using property files

The previous recipe taught us about the application properties and how they are provisioned. As was mentioned in the beginning of this chapter, during application deployment, it is almost inevitable to have some property values that are environment dependant. They can be database configurations, service topologies, or even simple feature configurations where something might be enabled in development but not quite ready for production just yet.

In this recipe, we will learn how to use an externally residing properties file for an environment-specific configuration, which might reside in the local filesystem or out in the wild on the Internet.

In this recipe, we will use the same application with all the existing configurations as we did in the previous recipe. We will use it to see how to consume external properties when we launch our application using the external configuration properties that are living in the local filesystem and from an Internet URL, such as GitHub or any other.

How to do it...

1. Let's start by adding a bit of code to log the value of our particular configuration property so that we can easily see the change in it as we do different things. Add an `@Bean` method to the `BookPubApplication` class located in the `src/main/java/org/test/bookpub` directory at the root of our project with the following content:

    ```
    @Bean
    public CommandLineRunner configValuePrinter(
      @Value("${my.config.value:}") String configValue) {
      return args -> LogFactory.getLog(getClass()).
        info("Value of my.config.value property is: " +
          configValue);
    }
    ```

2. Let's build the application by running `./gradlew clean bootRepackage` and start it by running `./build/libs/bookpub-0.0.1-SNAPSHOT-exec.jar --spring.profiles.active=logger` so as to see the following log output:

    2015-05-31 --- ication$$EnhancerBySpringCGLIB$$b123df6a : Value of my.config.value property is:

3. The value is empty as we expected. Next, we will create a file named `external.properties` in our home directly with the following content:

    my.config.value=From Home Directory Config

4. Let's run our application by executing `./build/libs/bookpub-0.0.1-SNAPSHOT-exec.jar --spring.profiles.active=logger --spring.config.location=file:/home/<username>/external.properties` in order to see the following output in the logs:

   ```
   2015-05-31 --- ication$$EnhancerBySpringCGLIB$$b123df6a : Value of
   my.config.value property is: From Home Directory Config
   ```

    For OS X users, the home directories can be found in the `/Users/<username>` folder.

5. We can also load the file as an HTTP resource and not from the local filesystem. So, place a file named `external.properties` with the content of `my.config.value=From HTTP Config` somewhere on the web. It can even be checked in a GitHub or BitBucket repository, as long as it is accessible without any need for authentication.

6. Let's run our application by executing `./build/libs/bookpub-0.0.1-SNAPSHOT-exec.jar --spring.profiles.active=logger --spring.config.location=http://<your file location path>/external.properties` in order to see the following output in the logs:

   ```
   2015-05-31 --- ication$$EnhancerBySpringCGLIB$$b123df6a : Value of
   my.config.value property is: From HTTP Config
   ```

How it works...

Before delving into the details of an external configuration setup, let's quickly look at the code that was added in order to print the property value in the log. The element of focus is the `@Value` annotation that can be used on class fields or method arguments; it also instructs Spring to automatically inject the annotated variable with the value defined in the annotation. If the value is positioned in the wrapping curly braces prefixed with a dollar sign, (`${ }`), Spring will replace this with the value from the corresponding application property or with the default value if it is provided by adding the textual data after the colon (:).

In our case, we defined it as `@Value("${my.config.value:}") String configValue;` so unless an application property named `my.config.value` exists, the default value of an empty String will be assigned to the `configValue` method argument. This construct is quite handy and eliminates the need to explicitly wire in the instance of an `Environment` object just to get a specific property value out of it as well as simplifies the code during the testing with less objects to mock.

The support for being able to specify the location of the application properties configuration file is geared towards supporting the dynamic multitude of environmental topologies, especially in cloud environments. This is often the case when the compiled application gets bundled into different cloud images that are destined for different environments and are being specially assembled by deployment tools such as Packer, Vagrant, and others.

In this scenario, it is very common to drop a configuration file in the image filesystem while making the image, depending on which environment it should be destined for. Spring Boot provides a very convenient ability to specify via the command-line arguments where the configuration properties file that should be added to the Application Configuration bundle resides.

Using the `--spring.config.location` start up option, we can specify a location of one or multiple files, which would then be separated by a comma (,), to be added to the default ones. The file designations can be either files from a local filesystem, a classpath, or a remote URL. The locations will be resolved either by the `DefaultResourceLoader` class or, if configured via a `SpringApplication` constructor or setter, by the implementation that is provided by the `SpringApplication` instance.

If the location contains directories, the names should end with a (/) so as to let Spring Boot know that it should look for the `application.properties` file in these directories.

If you want to change the default name of the file, Spring Boot provides us with this ability as well. Just set the `--spring.config.name` option to whatever file name that you want.

It is important to remember that the default search paths for the configuration of `classpath:`, `classpath:/config`, `file:`, `file:config/` will always be used regardless of the presence of the `--spring.config.location` setting. This way, you can always retain your default configuration in `application.properties` and just override the ones that you need via the start up settings.

Externalizing environmental config using environment variables

In the previous recipes, we have a number of times eluded to the fact that the configuration values to a Spring Boot application can be passed and overridden by using OS Environment Variables. Operating Systems rely on these variables to store information about various things. We probably have come across having to set `JAVA_HOME` or `PATH` a few times and these would be the examples of environment variables. It is also a very important feature in case one deploys their application using a PaaS Platform such as Heroku or Amazon AWS. In these environments, configuration values such as database access credentials and various API tokens are all provided over the environment variables.

Their power comes from the ability to completely externalize the configuration of simple key-value data pairs without the need to rely on placing a property or some other files in a particular location and having this hard-coded in the application codebase. These variables are also agnostic to the particular operating system and can be consumed in the Java program in the same way, `System.getenv()`, regardless of which OS the program is running on.

In this recipe, we will explore how this power can be leveraged to pass the configuration properties to our Spring Boot applications. We will continue to use the codebase from the previous recipe and experiment with a few different ways of starting the application and using the OS environment variables in order to change the configuration values of some properties.

How to do it...

1. In the previous recipe, we added a configuration property named `my.config.value`. Let's build the application by running `./gradlew clean bootRepackage` and start it by running `MY_CONFIG_VALUE="From ENV Config" ./build/libs/bookpub-0.0.1-SNAPSHOT-exec.jar --spring.profiles.active=logger` so as to see the following output in the logs:

    ```
    2015-05-31 --- ication$$EnhancerBySpringCGLIB$$b123df6a : Value of
    my.config.value property is: From ENV Config
    ```

2. If we want to use the environment variables while running our application via the Gradle `bootRun` task, the command line will be `MY_CONFIG_VALUE="From ENV Config" ./gradlew clean bootRun` and should produce the same output as in the preceding step.

3. Conveniently enough, we can even mix and match how we set the configurations. We can use the environment variable to configure the `spring.config.location` property and use it to load other property values from the external properties file as we did in the previous recipe. Let's try this by launching our application by executing `SPRING_CONFIG_LOCATION=file:/home/<username>/external.properties ./gradlew bootRun`. We should see the following in the logs:

    ```
    2015-05-31 --- ication$$EnhancerBySpringCGLIB$$b123df6a : Value of
    my.config.value property is: From Home Directory Config
    ```

> While using environment variables is very convenient, it does have a maintenance overhead if the number of these variables gets too many. To help deal with this issue, it is good practice to use the method of delegation by setting the `SPRING_CONFIG_LOCATION` variable to configure the location of the environment-specific properties file, typically by loading them from some URL location.

How it works...

As you learned from the section on *Spring Boot environment config hierarchy and precedence* in this chapter. Spring Boot offers multiple ways of providing the configuration properties. Each of these is managed via an appropriate `PropertySource` implementation. We have seen how to create a custom implementation of `PropertySource` when we were implementing `ApacheCommonsConfigurationPropertySource`. Spring Boot already provides a `SystemEnvironmentPropertySource` implementation for us to use out of the box. This even gets automatically registered with the default implementation of the environment interface: the `SystemEnvironment`.

As the `SystemEnvironment` implementation provides a composite façade on top of a multitude of different `PropertySource` implementations, the overriding takes place seamlessly, simply because the `SystemEnvironmentPropertySource` class sits higher up in the list than the `application.properties` file one.

An important aspect that you should notice is the use of **ALL_CAPS** with underscore (_) in order to separate the words instead of the traditional conventional `all.lower.cased` format with dots (.) separating the words used in Spring Boot to name the configuration properties. This is due to the nature of some Operating Systems, namely Linux and OS X, that prevents the use of dots (.) in the names and instead encourages the use of the **ALL_CAPS** underscore-separated notation

In situations where the usage of environment variables to specify or override the configuration properties is not desired, Spring Boot provides us with `-Dspring.getenv.ignore` system property, which can be set to true, and prevents the usage of environment variables. One might want to change this setting to `true` if you see errors or exceptions in the log due to the running of your code on some application servers, or a particular security policy configuration that might not allow access to environment variables.

Externalizing environmental config using Java system properties

While environment variables could, on a rare occasion, be a hit or miss, the good old Java system properties can always be trusted to be there for you. In addition to using the Environment Variables and command-line arguments represented by the property names prefixed with a double dash (--), Spring Boot provides you with the ability to use the plain Java System Properties to set or override the configuration properties.

This could be useful in a number of situations, particularly if your application is running in a container that sets certain values during the startup via the system properties that you want to get access to or if a property value is not set via a command-line -D argument, but rather in some library via a code by calling `System.setProperty(...)`, especially if this resides in a static method of sorts. While arguably these cases are rare, it takes only one to have you bend backwards in an effort to try and integrate this value into your application.

In this recipe, we will use the same application executable binary as we have done in the previous recipe, with the only difference of using Java System Properties instead of the command-line arguments or Environment Variables to set our configuration properties at runtime.

How to do it...

1. Let's continue our experiments by setting the `my.config.value` configuration property. Build the application by running `./gradlew clean bootRepackage` and start it by running `java -Dmy.config.value="From System Config" -jar ./build/libs/bookpub-0.0.1-SNAPSHOT-exec.jar` so as to see the following in the logs:

   ```
   2015-05-31 --- ication$$EnhancerBySpringCGLIB$$b123df6a : Value of
   my.config.value property is: From System Config
   ```

2. If we want to be able to set the Java System Property while running our app using the Gradle's `bootRun` task, we will need to add this to the `applicationDefaultJvmArgs` configuration in the `build.gradle` file. Let's add `-Dmy.config.value=Gradle` to this list and start the application by running `./gradlew clean bootRun` and we should see the following in the logs:

   ```
   2015-05-31 --- ication$$EnhancerBySpringCGLIB$$b123df6a : Value of
   my.config.value property is: Gradle
   ```

3. As we made the `applicationDefaultJvmArgs` setting to be shared with `launch.script`, rebuilding the application by running `./gradlew clean bootRepackage` and starting it by running `./build/libs/bookpub-0.0.1-SNAPSHOT-exec.jar` should yield us the same output in the logs as in the preceding step.

How it works...

You might have already guessed that Java System Properties are consumed by a similar mechanism that is used for environment variables, and you would be correct. The only real difference is the implementation of `PropertySource`. This time, a more generic `MapPropertySource` implementation is used by `StandardEnvironment`.

What you have also probably noticed is the need to launch our application using the `java -Dmy.config.value="From System Config" -jar ./build/libs/bookpub-0.0.1-SNAPSHOT-exec.jar` command instead of just simply invoking the self-executing packaged jar by itself. This is because, unlike the Environment Variables and command-line arguments, Java System Properties have to be set on the `java` executable ahead of everything else.

We did manage to work around this need by effectively hard-coding the values in our `build.gradle` file, which, combined with the enhancements that we made to `launch.script`, allowed us embed the `my.config.value` property in the command line in the self-executing jar as well as use it with the Gradle's `bootRun` task.

The risk of using this approach with the configuration properties is that it will always override the values that we set in the higher layers of the configuration, such as `application.properties` and others. Unless you are explicitly constructing the `java` executable command line and not using the self-launching capabilities of the packaged JAR, it is best not to use Java System Properties and consider using the command-line arguments or environment variables instead.

Setting up Consul

So far, everything that we have been doing with the configuration was connected to the local set of data. In a real large-scale enterprise environment, this is not always the case and quite frequently, there is a desire to be able to make the configuration changes at large—across hundreds or even thousands of instances or machines.

There are a number of tools that exist to help you with this task, and in this recipe, we will take a look at one that—in my opinion—stands out from the group, giving you the ability to cleanly and elegantly configure the environment variables for a starting application using a distributed data store. The tool's name is **Consul**. It is an open source product from Hashicorp and is designed to discover and configure the services in a large, distributed infrastructure.

In this recipe, we will take a look at how to install and do the basic configuration of Consul, and experiment with some key functionalities that it provides. This will give us the necessary familiarity for our next recipe, where we will be using Consul to provide the configuration values that are needed to start our application.

How to do it...

1. Go to `https://consul.io/downloads.html` and download the appropriate archive, depending on the operating system that you are using. Consul supports Windows, OS X, and Linux, so it should work for the majority of the readers.

> If you are an OS X user, you can install Consul using Homebrew by running `brew install caskroom/cask/brew-cask` followed by `brew cask install consul`.

2. After the installation, we should be able to run `consul --version` and see the following output:

```
Consul v0.5.2

Consul Protocol: 2 (Understands back to: 1)
```

3. With Consul successfully installed, we should be able to start it by running `consul agent -server -bootstrap-expect 1 -data-dir /tmp/consul` and our terminal window will display the following:

```
==> WARNING: BootstrapExpect Mode is specified as 1; this is the
same as Bootstrap mode.

==> WARNING: Bootstrap mode enabled! Do not enable unless
necessary

==> WARNING: It is highly recommended to set GOMAXPROCS higher
than 1

==> Starting Consul agent...

==> Starting Consul agent RPC...

==> Consul agent running!

        Node name: <your machine name>'

        Datacenter: 'dc1'

            Server: true (bootstrap: true)

        Client Addr: 127.0.0.1 (HTTP: 8500, HTTPS: -1, DNS: 8600,
RPC: 8400)

        Cluster Addr: 192.168.1.227 (LAN: 8301, WAN: 8302)

    Gossip encrypt: false, RPC-TLS: false, TLS-Incoming: false

            Atlas: <disabled>


==> Log data will now stream in as it occurs:


    2015/06/10 20:34:43 [INFO] serf: EventMemberJoin: <your
machine name> 192.168.1.227
```

```
      2015/06/10 20:34:43 [INFO] serf: EventMemberJoin: <your
machine name>.dc1 192.168.1.227

      2015/06/10 20:34:43 [INFO] raft: Node at 192.168.1.227:8300
[Follower] entering Follower state

      2015/06/10 20:34:43 [INFO] consul: adding server <your machine
name> (Addr: 192.168.1.227:8300) (DC: dc1)

      2015/06/10 20:34:43 [INFO] consul: adding server <your machine
name>.dc1 (Addr: 192.168.1.227:8300) (DC: dc1)

      2015/06/10 20:34:43 [ERR] agent: failed to sync remote state:
No cluster leader

      2015/06/10 20:34:45 [WARN] raft: Heartbeat timeout reached,
starting election

      2015/06/10 20:34:45 [INFO] raft: Node at 192.168.1.227:8300
[Candidate] entering Candidate state

      2015/06/10 20:34:45 [INFO] raft: Election won. Tally: 1

      2015/06/10 20:34:45 [INFO] raft: Node at 192.168.1.227:8300
[Leader] entering Leader state

      2015/06/10 20:34:45 [INFO] consul: cluster leadership acquired

      2015/06/10 20:34:45 [INFO] consul: New leader elected: <your
machine name>

      2015/06/10 20:34:45 [INFO] raft: Disabling EnableSingleNode
(bootstrap)

      2015/06/10 20:34:45 [INFO] consul: member '<your machine
name>' joined, marking health alive

      2015/06/10 20:34:47 [INFO] agent: Synced service 'consul'
```

4. With the Consul service running, we can verify that it contains one member by running `consul members` command and should see the following result:

```
Node            Address              Status  Type   Build Protocol
DC

<your_machine_name>  192.168.1.227:8301  alive   server 0.5.2  2
dc1
```

5. While Consul can also provide discovery for services, health checks, distributed locks, and more, we are going to focus on the Key/Value service as this is what will be used to provide the configuration in the next recipe. So, let's put the `From Consul Config` value in the **KV** store by executing `curl -X PUT -d 'From Consul Config'` `http://localhost:8500/v1/kv/bookpub/my/config/value`.

If you are using Windows, you can get cURL from `http://curl.haxx.se/download.html`.

6. We can also retrieve the data by running `curl http://localhost:8500/v1/kv/bookpub/my/config/value` and should see the following output:

   ```
   [{"CreateIndex":20,"ModifyIndex":20,"LockIndex":0,"Key":"bookpub/
   my/config/value","Flags":0,"Value":"RnJvbSBDb25zdWwgQ29uZmln"}]
   ```

7. We can delete this value by running `curl -X DELETE http://localhost:8500/v1/kv/bookpub/my/config/value`.

8. In order to modify the existing value for something else, execute `curl -X PUT -d 'newval' http://localhost:8500/v1/kv/bookpub/my/config/value?cas=20`.

How it works...

The detailed explanation about how Consul works or about all the possible options for its **Key/Value** service would take a book of its own, so here we will look only at the basic pieces and it is strongly recommended that you read the Consul's documentation at `https://consul.io/intro/getting-started/services.html`.

In Step 3, we started the Consul agent in a server mode. It acts as a main master node and in the real deployment, the local agents running on the individual instances will be using the server node to connect to and retrieve data from. For our test purpose, we will just use this server node as if it were a local agent one.

The information displayed upon the startup shows us that our node has started as a server node, establishing an HTTP service on port 8500 as well as the DNS and RPC services, in case that's how one chooses to connect to it. We can also see that there is only one node in the cluster—ours—and we are the elected leader running in a healthy state.

As we will be using the convenient RESTful HTTP API via cURL, all of our requests will be using localhost on port 8500. Being a RESTful API, it fully adheres to a CRUD verb terminology and to insert the data, we will use a PUT method on a `/v1/kv` endpoint in order to set the `bookpub/my/config/value` key.

Retrieving the data is even more straightforward: we just make a GET request to the same `/v1/kv` service using the desired key. The same goes for DELETE, with the only difference being the method name.

The update operation requires a bit more information in the URL, namely the `cas` parameter. The value of this parameter should be `ModifyIndex` of the desired key, which can be obtained from the GET request. In our case, it has a value of 20.

Externalizing environmental config using Consul and envconsul

In the previous recipe, we had our Consul service installed and experimented with its **Key/Value** capabilities to learn how we can manipulate the data in it. Next step would be to integrate Consul with our application and make the data extraction process seamless and non-invasive from the application's stand point.

As we don't want our application to know anything about Consul and have to explicitly connect to it—even though such a possibility exists—we will employ another utility, also created and open-sourced by Hashicorp, called envconsul to connect to the Consul service for us, extract the specified configuration key/value tree, and expose it as the environment variables to be used while also launching our application. Pretty cool, right?!

Getting ready

Before we get started with launching our application that was created in the previous recipes, we need to install the envconsul utility.

Let's download the binary for your respective operating system from `https://github.com/hashicorp/envconsul/releases` and extract the executable to any directory of your choice; though it is better to put it somewhere that is in the PATH.

Once envconsul is extracted from the downloaded archive, we are ready to start using it so as to configure our application.

How to do it...

1. If you have not already added the value for the `my/config/value` key to Consul, let's add it by running `curl -X PUT -d 'From Consul Config' http://localhost:8500/v1/kv/bookpub/my/config/value`.

2. The first step is to make sure envconsul can connect to the Consul server and that it extracts the correct data based on our configuration key. Let's execute a simple test by running `envconsul --once --sanitize --upcase --prefix bookpub env` and we should see the following in the output:

   ```
   ...
   TERM=xterm-256color
   SHELL=/bin/bash
   LANG=en_US.UTF-8
   HOME=/Users/<your_user_name>
   ...
   MY_CONFIG_VALUE=From Consul Config
   ```

3. After we have verified that envconsul is returning the correct data to us, we will use it to launch our `BookPub` application by running `envconsul --once --sanitize --upcase --prefix bookpub ./gradlew clean bootRun` and once the application has started, we should see the following output in the logs:

    ```
    2015-05-31 --- ication$$EnhancerBySpringCGLIB$$b123df6a : Value of
    my.config.value property is: From Consul Config
    ```

4. We can do the same thing by building the self-starting executable JAR by running `./gradlew clean bootRepackage` and start it by running `envconsul --once --sanitize --upcase --prefix bookpub ./build/libs/bookpub-0.0.1-SNAPSHOT-exec.jar` to make sure we see the same output in the logs as in the preceding step. If you see `Gradle` instead of `From Consul Config`, make sure the `applicationDefaultJvmArgs` configuration in `build.gradle` does not have `-Dmy.config.value=Gradle` in it.

5. Another marvelous ability of envconsul is not only to export the configuration key values as environment variables, but also monitor for any changes and restart the application if the values in Consul change. Let's launch our application by running `envconsul --sanitize --upcase --prefix bookpub ./build/libs/bookpub-0.0.1-SNAPSHOT-exec.jar` and we should see the following value in the log:

    ```
    2015-05-31 --- ication$$EnhancerBySpringCGLIB$$b123df6a : Value of
    my.config.value property is: From Consul Config
    ```

6. We will now use the `curl` command to get the current `ModifyIndex` of our key and update its value to `From UpdatedConsul Config` by opening another terminal window and executing `curl http://localhost:8500/v1/kv/bookpub/my/config/value`, grabbing the `ModifyIndex` value, and using it to execute `curl -X PUT -d 'From UpdatedConsul Config' http://localhost:8500/v1/kv/bookpub/my/config/value?cas=<ModifyIndex Value>`. We should see our running application magically restart itself and our newly updated value displayed in the log at the end:

    ```
    2015-05-31 --- ication$$EnhancerBySpringCGLIB$$b123df6a : Value of
    my.config.value property is: From UpdatedConsul Config
    ```

How it works...

What we just did was pretty sweet, right!? Let's examine the magic behind the scenes in more detail. We will start by dissecting the command line and explaining what each argument control option does.

Our first execution command line was `envconsul --once --sanitize --upcase --prefix bookpub ./gradlew clean bootRun`, so let's take a look at exactly what we did, as follows:

- First, one might notice that there is no indication as to which Consul node we should be connecting to. This is because there is an implicit understanding or an assumption that you already have a Consul agent running locally on *localhost:8500*. If this is not the case for whatever reason, you can always explicitly specify the Consul instance to connect via the `--consul localhost:8500` argument added to the command line.

- The `--prefix` option specifies the starting configuration key segment in which to look for the different values. When we were adding keys to Consul, we used the following key: `bookpub/my/config/value`. By specifying the `--prefix bookpub` option, we tell envconsul to strip the `bookpub` part of the key and use all the internal tree elements in `bookpub` to construct the environment variables. Thus, `my/config/value` becomes the environment variable.

- The `--sanitize` option tells envconsul to replace all the invalid characters with underscores (_). So, if we were to only use `--sanitize`, we would end up with `my_config_value` as an environment variable.

- The `--upcase` option, as you might already have guessed, makes the environment variable key to all upper cased characters; so, when combined with the `--sanitize`, `my/config/value` key, it gets transformed into the `MY_CONFIG_VALUE` environment variable.

- The `--once` option indicates that we only want to externalize the keys as environment variables once and do not want to continuously monitor for changes in the Consul cluster, and if a key in our prefix tree has changed its value, re-externalize the keys as environment variables and restart the application.

This last option, `--once`, provides a very useful choice of functionalities. If you are interested only in the initial bootstrap of your application via the use of a Consul-shared configuration, then the keys will be set as environment variables, application will be launched, and envconsul will consider its job done. However, if you would like to monitor the Consul cluster for changes to key/values and after the change has taken place, restart your application reflecting the new change, then by removing the `--once` option, envconsul will restart the application once the change has occurred.

Such a behavior can be very useful and handy for things such as a near-instantaneous change to the database connection configuration. Imagine that you need to do a quick failover from one database to another and JDBC URL is configured via Consul. All you need to do is push a new JDBC URL value and envconsul will almost immediately detect this change and restart the application telling it to connect to a new database node.

Currently, this functionality is implemented by sending a traditional SIGTERM signal to an application running process telling it to terminate and once the process exited, restart the application. This might not always be the desired behavior, especially if it takes some time for an application to start up and be capable of taking traffic. You don't want your entire cluster of web applications to be shut down, even if it will be only for a few minutes.

To provide a better handling of this scenario, envconsul was enhanced to be able to send a number of standard signals that can be configured via a newly added `--kill-signal` option. Using this option, we can specify any of the SIGHUP, SIGTERM, SIGINT, SIGQUIT, SIGUSR1, or SIGUSR2 signals to be used instead of the default SIGTERM to be sent to a running application process once the key/value changes have been detected. This functionality should become available as of version 0.5.1 or 0.6, whichever's release comes first.

The process signal handling in Java is not as clear and straightforward due to most of the behavior being very specific to a particular operating system and the JVM that is run atop. Some of the signals in the list will terminate the application anyways or, in the case of SIGQUIT, the JVM will print Core Dump into the standard output. However, there are ways to configure the JVM, depending on the operating system, to let us use SIGUSR1 and SIGUSR2 instead of acting on those signals itself, but unfortunately that topic falls outside the scope of this book.

Here is a sample example of how to deal with Signal Handlers: `https://github.com/spotify/daemon-java` or see Oracle Java documentation at `https://docs.oracle.com/javase/8/docs/technotes/guides/troubleshoot/signals.html` for a detailed explanation.

7
Health Monitoring and Data Visualization

In this chapter, you will learn about the following topics:

- ▶ Writing custom health indicators
- ▶ Emitting metrics
- ▶ Monitoring Spring Boot via JMX
- ▶ Management of Spring Boot via CRaSH and writing custom remote shell commands
- ▶ Integrating Codahale/Dropwizard metrics with Graphite
- ▶ Integrating Codahale/Dropwizard metrics with Dashing

Introduction

In the previous chapter, you learned a few techniques about how to efficiently package and get the application ready for deployment, as well as a number of techniques to provide an environmental configuration without changing the code. With the deployment and configuration woes behind us, the last but not least, important step remains: ensuring that we have complete visibility, monitoring, and management control of our application, as it is running in the production environment and is exposed to the harsh environment of customers' (ab)use.

Just as airline pilots don't like to fly blind, neither do developers get excited if they can't see how their beloved and hard-worked-on application performs in production. We want to know, at any given time, how the CPU utilization is doing, how much memory we are consuming, is our connection to the database up and available, how many customers use the system in any given time interval, and so on and so forth. Not only do we want to know all these things, but we also want to be able to see it in pretty charts, graphs, and visual dashboards. These come in very handy to put on the big *Plasma* displays to monitor as well as impress your boss so as to show that you are on top of things and have everything under control.

This chapter will help us learn the necessary techniques to enhance our application in order to expose custom metrics, health status, and so on, as well as how to get the monitoring data out of our application and either store it in Graphite for historical reference or use this data to create real-time monitoring dashboards using the Dashing and Grafana frameworks. We will also take a look at the capabilities to connect to running instances and perform various management tasks using the powerful CRaSH framework integration.

 While this chapter was being written, various changes to the 1.3.0-SNAPSHOT version of Spring Boot have been added; one of them is the rendering output of JSON to be more HATEOAS compliant.

Writing custom health indicators

Knowing the state of the application that is running in the production, especially in a large-scale distributed system, is just as—if not more—important than having things such as automated testing and deployment. In today's fast paced IT world, we can't really afford much downtime, so we need to have the information about the health of the application at our fingertips, ready to go at a minute's notice. If the all-so-important database connections go down, we want to see it right away and be able to quickly remedy the situation; the customers are not going to be waiting around for long before they go to another site.

We will resume working on our `BookPub` application in the state as we left it in the previous chapter. In this recipe, we will add the necessary Spring Boot starters to enable the monitoring and instrumentation of our application and will even write our own health indicator.

How to do it...

1. The first thing that we need to do is add a dependency on the Spring Boot Actuator starter in our `build.gradle` file with the following content:

```
dependencies {
    ...
    compile("org.springframework.boot:spring-boot-starter-data-
rest")
```

```
    // compile("org.springframework.boot:spring-boot-starter-
jetty") // Need to use Jetty instead of Tomcat
    compile("org.springframework.boot:spring-boot-starter-
actuator")
    compile project(':db-count-starter')

    ...
}
```

2. Adding this dependency alone already gives us an ability to access the Spring management endpoints, such as /env, /info, /metrics, /health, and so on. So, let's start our application by executing ./gradlew clean bootRun and then we can access the newly available /health endpoint by opening our browser and going to http://localhost:8080/health in the browser so as to see the new endpoint in action, as shown in the following screenshot:

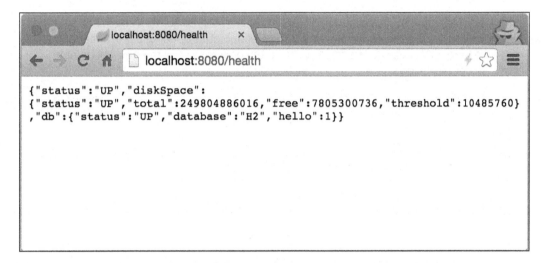

3. With the Actuator dependency added, we can now add and perform all kinds of monitoring functions on our application. Let's go ahead and populate the /info endpoint with some data by adding the property placeholders to application. properties located in the src/main/resources directory at the root of our project with the following content:

```
info.build.name=${name}
info.build.description=${description}
info.build.version=${version}
```

4. Next, we will create a new properties file named gradle.properties in the root directory of our project with the following content:

```
version=0.0.1-SNAPSHOT
description=BookPub Catalog Application
```

5. We will also add `rootProject.name='BookPub'` to the `settings.gradle` file located in the root directory of our project.

6. To stitch things together, we will enhance `build.gradle` with the following configuration:

```
bootRun {
    addResources = false
}

processResources {
    filesMatching("**/application.properties") {
        expand(project.properties)
    }
}
```

7. Now, let's start our application by executing `./gradlew clean bootRun` and then we can access the newly available `/info` endpoint by opening our browser and going to `http://localhost:8080/info` in the browser to see the new endpoint in action, as follows:

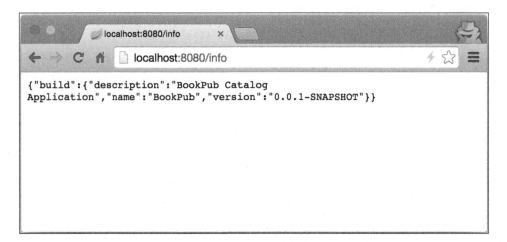

8. As we have got the hang of how things work, let's go ahead and make our custom health indicator, which will be accessible via the `/health` endpoint, in order to report the count status of the entries for each of our repositories. If they are greater or equal to `0`, we are UP, otherwise we are not really sure what's going on. Obviously, if an exception has occurred, we would be reporting DOWN. Let's start by relaxing the `getRepositoryName(...)` method visibility from `private` to `protected` in `DbCountRunner.java` located in the `db-count-starter/src/main/java/org/test/bookpubstarter/dbcount` directory at the root of our project.

9. Next, we will add the same dependency on the `compile("org.springframework.boot:spring-boot-starter-actuator")` library to `build.gradle` in the `db-count-starter` directory at the root of our project.

10. Now, we will create a new file named `DbCountHealthIndicator.java` in the `db-count-starter/src/main/java/org/test/bookpubstarter/dbcount` directory at the root of our project with the following content:

```
public class DbCountHealthIndicator implements HealthIndicator {
    private CrudRepository repository;

    public DbCountHealthIndicator(CrudRepository repository) {
        this.repository = repository;
    }

    @Override
    public Health health() {
        try {
            long count = repository.count();
            if (count >= 0) {
                return Health.up().
                    withDetail("count", count).build();
            } else {
                return Health.unknown().
                    withDetail("count", count).build();
            }
        } catch (Exception e) {
            return Health.down(e).build();
        }
    }
}
```

11. Finally, for the automatic registration of our `HealthIndicator`, we will enhance `DbCountAutoConfiguration.java` located in the `db-count-starter/src/main/java/org/test/bookpubstarter/dbcount` directory at the root of our project with the following content:

```
@Autowired
private HealthAggregator healthAggregator;
@Bean
public HealthIndicator dbCountHealthIndicator(
  Collection<CrudRepository> repositories) {
    CompositeHealthIndicator compositeHealthIndicator =
      new CompositeHealthIndicator(healthAggregator);
    for (CrudRepository repository : repositories) {
        String name = DbCountRunner.getRepositoryName(repository.
getClass());
```

```
        compositeHealthIndicator.addHealthIndicator(name,
            new DbCountHealthIndicator(repository));
    }
    return compositeHealthIndicator;
}
```

12. So, let's start our application by executing `./gradlew clean bootRun` and then we can access the `/health` endpoint by opening our browser and going to `http://localhost:8080/health` in the browser to see our new `HealthIndicator` in action, as follows:

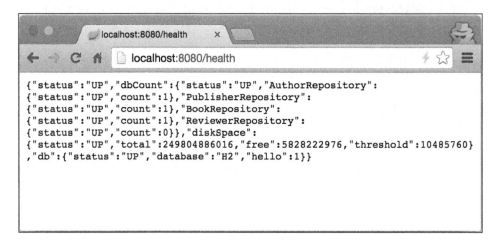

How it works...

The Spring Boot Actuator starter adds a number of important features that give insight into the runtime state of the application. The library contains a number of **AutoConfigurations** that add and configure the various endpoints to access the runtime monitoring data and health of the application. The following endpoints are available to aid us in getting insight into the application runtime state and configuration:

> The `/env` endpoint provides us with the ability to query the application about all of the environment variables that the application has access to via the environment implementation, which we have seen earlier. It is very useful when you need to debug a particular issue and want to know a value of any given configuration property. If we access the endpoint by going to `http://localhost:8080/env`, we will see a number of different configuration sections, for example, class path resource `[tomcat.https.properties]`, `applicationConfig: [classpath:/ application.properties]`, `commonsConfig`, `systemEnvironment`, `systemProperties`, and others.

They all represent an instance of an individual `PropertySource` implementation that is available in the `Environment` instance and depending on their place in the hierarchy, may or may not be used to provide the value resolution at the runtime. To find out exactly which entry is used to resolve a particular value, for example, for the `book.count.rate` property, we can query it by going to the `http://localhost:8080/env/book.counter.rate` URL and by default, should get 10000 as a result, unless of course, a different value was set via the system environment or command-line arguments as an override. If you really want to dig deep in the code, the `EnvironmentEndpoint` class is responsible for handling the logic behind this capability.

- The `/configprops` endpoint provides you with an insight into the settings of the various configuration property objects, such as our `WebConfiguration.TomcatSslConnectorProperties` one. It is slightly different from the `/env` endpoint as it provides insight into the configuration object bindings. If we open the browser to go to `http://localhost:8080/configprops` and search for `custom.tomcat.https`, we will see the entry for our configuration property object that we will use to configure `TomcatSslConnector`, which was automatically populated and bound for us by Spring Boot.

- The `/autoconfig` endpoint serves as a web-based analog to AutoConfiguration Report, which we have seen in *Chapter 4, Writing Custom Spring Boot Starters*. This way, we can get the report using the browser at any time without having to start the application with the specific flags to get it printed.

- The `/beans` endpoint is designed to list all the beans that have been created by Spring Boot and are available in Application Context.

- The `/mappings` endpoint exposes a list of all the URL mappings that are supported by the application as well as a reference to the `HandlerMapping` bean implementation. This is very useful to answer a question of *where would a specific URL get routed to*. Try going to `http://localhost:8080/mappings` to see the list of all the routes that our application can handle.

- The `/info` endpoint shows the basic description and application information that we added and we've seen this in action, so it should be familiar to us as of now. The nice support in the build tools gives us the ability to replace the data placeholders in `application.properties` with the real values using the `processResources` directive, which expands the project properties to `application.properties`, thus allowing us to automatically populate the placeholders with the current data at all times.

Any properties that start with info. will be displayed while accessing the `/info` endpoint, so you are definitely not limited to only the three endpoints that we used previously. Configuring this specific endpoint in order to return the relevant information can be very helpful when building various automated discovery and monitoring tools as it is a great way to expose application-specific information in the form of a nice JSON RESTful API.

- ▶ The /health endpoint provides information about the general application health status as well as a detailed breakdown and health status of the individual components.

- ▶ The /metrics endpoint gives an overview of all the various data points that are emitted by the Metrics subsystem. You can experiment with it by accessing it via the http://localhost:8080/metrics URL in the browser. We will cover this in more detail in the next recipe.

Now that we know in general what is being provided for us by Spring Boot Actuator, we can move on to take a look at the details of what we did to get our custom HealthIndicator working and how the whole Health monitoring subsystem in Spring Boot functions.

As you saw, getting the basic HealthIndicator to work is very easy: all we have to do is create an implementing class that will return a Health object upon a call to the health() method. All you have to do is expose the instance of the HealthIndicator as @Bean for Spring Boot to pick it up and add it to the /health endpoint.

In our case, we went a step further because we had to deal with the need to create a HealthIndicator for each CrudRepository instance. To accomplish this, we created an instance of CompositeHealthIndicator to which we added all the instances of DbHealthIndicator for each CrudRepository. We then returned this as @Bean and this is what was used by Spring Boot to represent the health status. Being a composite, it preserved the inner hierarchy as is evident from the returned JSON data representing the health status. We also added some extra data element to provide the indication of the entry count as well as the name of each particular repository so that we can tell them apart.

Looking at the code, you are probably wondering: *what is this HealthAggregator instance that we've wired in*. The reason that we needed a HealthAggregator instance is because CompositeHealthIndicator needs to know how to decide if the inner composition of all the nested HeathIndicators represents good or bad health as a whole. Imagine that all the repositories, but one, return UP, except for one, which returns DOWN. What does this mean: is the composite indicator healthy as a whole or should it also report DOWN because one inner repository is having issues?

By default, Spring Boot already creates and uses an instance of HealthAggregator, so we just @Autowired it and used it in our use case as well. Even though the default implementation is an instance of OrderedHealthAggregator, which just collects all the inner Status responses and chooses the lowest on the priority level out of DOWN, OUT_OF_SERVICE, UP, and UNKNOWN, it doesn't always have to be that way. For example, if the composite indicator consists of the indicators for redundant service connections, your combined result could be UP as long as at least one of the connections is healthy. Creating a custom HealthAggregator is very easy: all one has to do is either extend AbstractHealthAggregator or implement a HealthAggregator interface itself.

Before we continue with the next recipe, I wanted to touch briefly on the topic of the Spring Boot Actuator endpoints and Security. The data that is exposed by the various management endpoints, especially the ones from sensitive ones such as `/health`, `/env`, and others, can be a very lucrative prize for malicious people on the outside. To prevent this from happening, Spring Boot provides us with an ability to configure if we want the endpoints to be available via `endpoints.enabled=false`. We can specify which individual endpoints we want to disable by setting an appropriate `endpoints.<name>.enabled=false` property as well.

Alternatively, we can set `management.port=-1` to disable the HTTP exposure of these endpoints or use a different port number in order to have the management endpoints and live services on different ports. If we want to enable access via only a localhost, we can achieve this by configuring `management.address=127.0.0.1` to prevent external access. Even the context URL path can be configured to something else, say `/admin`, via `management.context-path=/admin`. This way, to get access to a `/health` endpoint, we would go to `http://127.0.0.1/admin/health` instead. This can be useful if you want to control and restrict access via the firewall rules, so you can just add a filter to block external access to anything, `/admin/*`, for all the applications from the outside. With the addition of Spring Security, an authentication can also be configured to require a user login to get access to the endpoints.

Emitting metrics

The previous recipe has provided us with an overview of the capabilities provided by Spring Boot Actuators. We played with the different management endpoints such as `/info`, `/health`, and so on and even created our own health metrics to add to the default set. However, besides the health status there are a number of things that we, as developers and operations folks, want to be able to see and monitor on an ongoing basis, and just knowing that the uplink is functional is not good enough. We also would like to see the number of open sessions, concurrent requests to the application, latency, and so on and so forth. In this recipe, we will learn about the metric reporting facilities in Spring Boot as well as how to add our own metrics and some quick and simple ways of visualizing them.

Getting ready

To help us visualize the metrics better, we will be using a great open source project, `spring-boot-admin`, located at `https://github.com/codecentric/spring-boot-admin`. It provides a simple web UI on top of the Spring Boot Actuators to give a nicer view of the various data.

We will create a simple admin application in Gradle using the instructions from `https://github.com/codecentric/spring-boot-admin#server-application` following these simple steps:

1. Go to `start.spring.io` and create a new application template with the following fields:

   ❑ **Group**: `org.sample.admin`

   ❑ **Artifact**: `spring-boot-admin-web`

   ❑ **Name**: `Spring Boot Admin Web`

   ❑ **Description**: `Spring Boot Admin Web Application`

   ❑ **Package Name**: `org.sample.admin`

   ❑ **Type**: `Gradle Project`

   ❑ **Packaging**: `Jar`

   ❑ **Java Version**: `1.8`

   ❑ **Language**: `Java`

   ❑ **Spring Boot Version**: `1.2.5`

2. Select the **Actuator** option in the **Ops** group.

3. Click **Generate Project** to download the application template archive.

4. Extract the contents in the directory of your choice.

5. In the extracted directory, execute `gradle wrapper` to generate a gradlew script.

6. In the `build.gradle` file, add the following dependencies to the dependencies block:

   ```
   compile("de.codecentric:spring-boot-admin-server:1.2.1")
   compile("de.codecentric:spring-boot-admin-server-ui:1.2.1")
   ```

7. Open `SpringBootAdminWebApplication.java` located in the `src/main/java/spring-boot-admin-web` directory and add the following annotations to the `SpringBootAdminWebApplication` class:

   ```
   @SpringBootApplication
   @EnableAdminServer
   public class SpringBootAdminWebApplication {

      public static void main(String[] args) {
        SpringApplication.run(SpringBootAdminWebApplication.class,
          args);
      }
   }
   ```

8. Open `application.properties` located in the `src/main/resources` directory and add the following settings:

```
server.port: 8090
spring.application.name: Spring Boot Admin Web
spring.boot.admin.url: http://localhost:${server.port}
spring.cloud.config.enabled: false
spring.jackson.serialization.indent_output: true
endpoints.health.sensitive: false
```

9. We are now ready to start our Admin Web Console by running `./gradlew bootRun` and open the browser to `http://localhost:8090` to see the following screenshot:

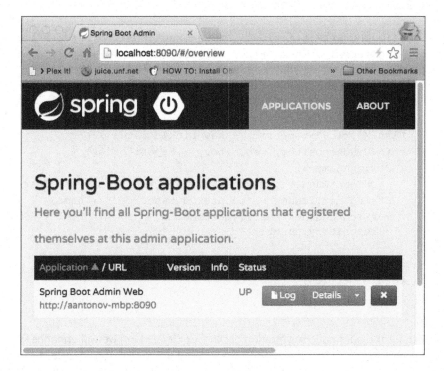

How to do it...

1. With the Admin Web up and running, we are now ready to start adding various metrics to our `BookPub` application. Let's expose the same information about our data repositories as we did in `HealthIndicators`, but this time, we will expose the counts data as `Metric`. We will continue to add code to our `db-count-starter` subproject. So, let's create a new file named `DbCountMetrics.java` in the `db-count-starter/src/main/java/org/test/bookpubstarter/dbcount` directory at the root of our project with the following content:

```java
public class DbCountMetrics implements PublicMetrics {
  private Collection<CrudRepository> repositories;

  public DbCountMetrics(Collection<CrudRepository> repositories) {
    this.repositories = repositories;
  }

  @Override
  public Collection<Metric<?>> metrics() {
    List<Metric<?>> metrics = new LinkedList<>();
    for (CrudRepository repository : repositories) {
      String name =
        DbCountRunner.getRepositoryName(repository.getClass());
      String metricName = "counter.datasource." + name;
      metrics.add(new Metric(metricName,
        repository.count()));

    }
    return metrics;
  }
}
```

2. Next, for the automatic registration of `DbCountMetrics`, we will enhance `DbCountAutoConfiguration.java` located in the `db-count-starter/src/main/java/org/test/bookpubstarter/dbcount` directory at the root of our project with the following content:

```java
@Bean
public PublicMetrics
  dbCountMetrics(Collection<CrudRepository> repositories) {
    return new DbCountMetrics(repositories);
}
```

3. So, let's start our application by executing `./gradlew clean bootRun` and then we can access the `/metrics` endpoint by opening our browser and going to `http://localhost:8080/metrics` in the browser to see our new `DbCountMetrics` added to the existing metrics list, as follows:

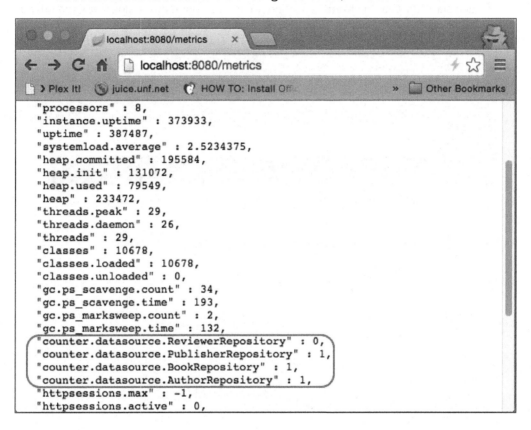

```
"processors" : 8,
"instance.uptime" : 373933,
"uptime" : 387487,
"systemload.average" : 2.5234375,
"heap.committed" : 195584,
"heap.init" : 131072,
"heap.used" : 79549,
"heap" : 233472,
"threads.peak" : 29,
"threads.daemon" : 26,
"threads" : 29,
"classes" : 10678,
"classes.loaded" : 10678,
"classes.unloaded" : 0,
"gc.ps_scavenge.count" : 34,
"gc.ps_scavenge.time" : 193,
"gc.ps_marksweep.count" : 2,
"gc.ps_marksweep.time" : 132,
"counter.datasource.ReviewerRepository" : 0,
"counter.datasource.PublisherRepository" : 1,
"counter.datasource.BookRepository" : 1,
"counter.datasource.AuthorRepository" : 1,
"httpsessions.max" : -1,
"httpsessions.active" : 0,
```

4. Our next step would be to get our application to appear in the Spring Boot Admin Web, which we created earlier. To make this happen, we will need to add a dependency on the `compile("de.codecentric:spring-boot-admin-starter-client:1.2.1")` library to `build.gradle` in the `db-count-starter` directory at the root of our project.

5. Additionally, `application.properties` located in the `src/main/resources` directory in the root of our project needs to be enhanced with the following entries:

```
spring.application.name=${description}
server.port=8080
spring.boot.admin.url=http://localhost:8090
```

6. Once again, let's start our application by executing `./gradlew clean bootRun` and if we now go to Spring Boot Admin Web by directing our browser to `http://localhost:8090`, we should see a new entry for our application named *BookPub Catalog Application* appear in the list. If we click on the **Details** button to the right and scroll down to the **Metrics** section, we will see our metrics along with the others, reported in a form of nicer looking horizontal green bars, as follows:

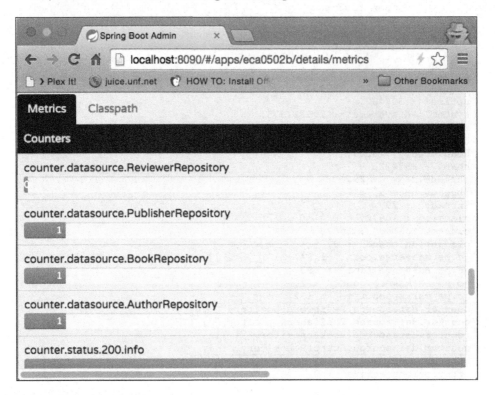

How it works...

A few words about Spring Boot Admin Web before we delve into the details of creating and emitting metrics. It is a simple web GUI that, in the backend, uses the same endpoints exposed by Spring Boot Actuator, which we learned about in the previous recipe. The data is extracted from the application as we click the various links in Admin Web and displayed in a nice graphical way—no magic!

We only had to configure a few properties in addition to adding the client library dependency in order to get our application to connect and register with Admin Web.

- ▶ `spring.application.name=${description}`: This configures the name of the application that we have chosen to take from the description property defined in `gradle.properties`. Admin Web uses this value when displaying the application list.

- ▶ `spring.boot.admin.url=http://localhost:8090`: This configures the location of the Admin Web application so that our application knows where to go in order to register itself. As we are running on port 8080, we chose to configure Admin Web to listen on port 8090, but any port can be chosen as desired. You can see more configuration options by visiting `https://github.com/codecentric/spring-boot-admin/blob/master/spring-boot-admin-starter-client/README.md`.

If we also want to enable the Logging Level control through the UI, we will need to add a Jolokia JMX library to our build dependency—`compile("org.jolokia:jolokia-core:+")`—as well as a `logback.xml` file in the `src/main/resources` directory in the root of the project with the following content:

```
<configuration>
  <include
    resource="org/springframework/boot/logging/logback/base.xml"/>
      <jmxConfigurator/>
</configuration>
```

The metrics facility in Spring Boot is very powerful and extendable, offering a number of different approaches to emit and consume metrics. Out of the box, Spring Boot already configures a number of data metrics that monitor the system resources, such as heap memory, thread counts, system uptime, and many others as well as the database usage and http session counts. The MVC endpoints are also instrumented to gauge the request latency, which is measured in milliseconds, as well as counter for each endpoint request status.

The gauge and counter metrics are emitted via the `GaugeService` and `CounterService` implementations that are provided by Spring Boot at runtime. These services can be easily autowired into any Spring-managed object and be used to emit metrics.

For example, we can easily count the number of times a particular method gets invoked by autowiring `CounterService` and placing the following line at the beginning of the method: `counterService.increment("objectName.methodName.invoked");`. Each time the method gets called, the particular metric count will get incremented.

This approach will give us the counts that we can increment, decrement, or reset, but if we want to measure latency or any other arbitrary value, we will need to use `GaugeService` to submit our metrics. To measure how long it will take for our method to execute, we can autowire `GaugeService` and at the beginning of the method, record the time: `long start = System.currentTimeMillis();`. We will then place our code and before the return, capture the time again: `long end = System.currentTimeMillis();`. Then we will emit the metric: `gaugeService.submit("objectName.methodName.latency", end - start);`, which will update the given metric with the latest value.

These services cover most of the simple use cases and are especially handy when we operate in our own code and have the flexibility to add them where we need to. However, it is not always the case and in these cases, we will need to resort to wrapping whatever it is we want to monitor by creating a custom implementation of `PublicMetrics`. In our case, we will use it to expose the counts for each of the repositories in the database as we can't insert any monitoring code into the `CrudRepository` proxy implementations.

The interface has only one method defined: `Collection<Metric<?>> metrics();`, which the implementer needs to code with the definition of what exactly is being monitored. The implementation class needs to be exposed as `@Bean` and it will automatically be picked up and registered with the `MetricsEndpoint` handler, which will execute the `metrics()` method every time the `/metrics` endpoint is being accessed.

Monitoring Spring Boot via JMX

In today's day and age, the RESTful HTTP JSON services are a de facto way of accessing data but this is not the only way to do so. Another quite popular and common way of managing systems in real time is via JMX. The good news is that Spring Boot already comes with the same level of support to expose the management endpoints over JMX as it does over HTTP. Actually, these are exactly the same endpoints; they are just wrapped around the MBean container.

In this recipe, we will take a look at how to retrieve the same information via JMX as we did via HTTP as well as how to expose some MBeans, which are provided by third-party libraries through HTTP using the Jolokia JMX library.

Getting ready

If you haven't done so already for the previous recipe, then please add the Jolokia JMX library to our `compile("org.jolokia:jolokia-core:+")` build dependency as we will need it to expose MBeans via HTTP.

How to do it...

1. After we add the Jolokia JMX dependency, all we need to do is build and start our application by executing `./gradlew clean bootRun` and now we can simply execute `jconsole` to see the the various endpoints exposed under the `org.springframework.boot` domain. The following is the screenshot:

2. After the Jolokia JMX library is added to the classpath, Spring Boot also enables the accessing of all the registered MBeans via HTTP API using the `/jolokia` endpoint. To find out the `maxThreads` setting for our Tomcat HTTP port 8080 connector, we can either look it up using jConsole by selecting the `maxThreads` attribute on `Tomcat:type=ThreadPool,name="http-nio-8080"` MBean to get the value of 200 or we can use Jolokia JMX HTTP by opening our browser and going to `http://localhost:8080/jolokia/read/Tomcat:type=ThreadPool,name=%22http-nio-8080%22/maxThreads` and we should see the following JSON response:

```
{"request":
  {"mbean":"Tomcat:name=\"http-nio-8080\",type=ThreadPool",
   "attribute":"maxThreads",
   "type":"read"
  },
  "value":200,"timestamp":1436740537,"status":200}
```

How it works...

By default, the Spring Boot Actuator, when added to the application, comes with all the endpoints and management services enabled. This includes the JMX access as well. If, for some reason, one would like to disable the exposing endpoints via JMX, this can easily be configured by adding `endpoints.jmx.enabled=false` or in order to disable the exporting of all the Spring MBeans, we can configure the `spring.jmx.enabled=false` setting in `application.properties`.

The presence of the Jolokia library in the classpath triggers Spring Boot `JolokiaAutoConfiguration`, which would automatically configure `JolokiaMvcEndpoint` accepting requests on `/jolokia` URL path. It is also possible to set various Jolokia-specific configuration options via `jolokia.config.*` set of properties. Complete list is available at `https://jolokia.org/reference/html/agents.html#agent-war-init-params`. In case you would like to use Jolokia, but want to manually set it up, we can tell Spring Boot to ignore it's presence by adding `endpoints.jolokia.enabled=false` setting in `application.properties`.

Management of Spring Boot via CRaSH and writing custom remote shell commands

Some of you are probably reminiscing about the good old days where all the administration was done via SSH directly on the machine, where one has complete flexibility and control, or even using a Telnet to connect to a management port and apply whatever the changes needed directly to a running application. For you, Spring Boot provides integration with the CRaSH Java Shell.

For this recipe, we will use the health indicator and management endpoint, which we created earlier in this chapter. We will expose the same capabilities via the SSH and Telnet console access.

How to do it...

1. The first step to get CRaSH to work is add the necessary dependency starters to our `build.gradle` file, as follows:

```
dependencies {
    ...
    compile("org.springframework.boot:spring-boot-starter-
actuator")
    compile("org.springframework.boot:spring-boot-starter-remote-
shell")
    compile("org.crashub:crash.connectors.telnet:1.3.1")
```

```
compile("de.codecentric:spring-boot-admin-starter-
  client:1.2.1")
compile("org.jolokia:jolokia-core:+")
...
}
```

2. Now, let's start our application by executing `./gradlew clean bootRun` and then connect to it via SSH by executing `ssh -p 2000 user@localhost`.

3. We will be prompted for a password so let's find the autogenerated hash key in the application startup log, which would look as follows:

   Using default password for shell access: 40c50992-ab6b-45f4-b17c-f8c8e5e94677

4. If the password is entered correctly, we will be greeted by the following welcome banner:

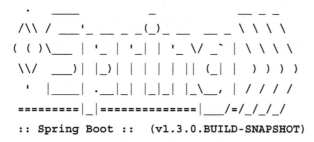

```
  .   ____          _            __ _ _
 /\\ / ___'_ __ _ _(_)_ __  __ _ \ \ \ \
( ( )\___ | '_ | '_| | '_ \/ _` | \ \ \ \
 \\/  ___)| |_)| | | | | || (_| |  ) ) ) )
  '  |____| .__|_| |_|_| |_\__, | / / / /
 =========|_|==============|___/=/_/_/_/
 :: Spring Boot ::   (v1.3.0.BUILD-SNAPSHOT)
```

5. Next, we will invoke our existing Health endpoint by typing `endpoint invoke healthEndpoint` and we should get the following result:

   {status=UP, dbCount={status=UP, PublisherRepository={status=UP, count=1}, ReviewerRepository={status=UP, count=0}, AuthorRepository={status=UP, count=1}, BookRepository={status=UP, count=1}}, diskSpace={status=UP, total=249804886016, free=2491744256, threshold=10485760}, db={status=UP, database=H2, hello=1}}

6. Typing `help` will show the list of all the existing commands so you can play with some of them to see what they do and then we will proceed with adding our own CRaSH command, which will enable us to add new publishers to the system via the command line.

7. Make a new directory named `commands` in `src/main/resources` at the root of our project.

8. Add a file named `publishers.groovy` in the `src/main/resources/commands` directory at the root of our project with the following content:

```
package commands

import org.crsh.cli.Option
```

```
import org.crsh.cli.Usage
import org.crsh.cli.Command
import org.crsh.command.InvocationContext
import org.springframework.beans.factory.BeanFactory
import org.test.bookpub.entity.Publisher
import org.test.bookpub.repository.PublisherRepository


@Usage("Publisher management")
class publishers {

    @Usage("Lists all publishers")
    @Command
    def list(InvocationContext context) {
        PublisherRepository repository =
                        getPublisherRepository(context)
        if (repository) {
            repository.findAll().each{publisher ->
                context.provide([id:publisher.id, name:publisher.
name])
            }
        } else {
            return "PublisherRepository is not found!"
        }
    }


    @Usage("Add new publisher")
    @Command
    def add(@Usage("publisher name") @Option(names=["n","name"])
String name, InvocationContext context) {
        PublisherRepository repository =
                            getPublisherRepository(context)
        if (repository) {
            publisher = new Publisher(name)
            try {
                publisher = repository.save(publisher)
                return "Added new publisher ${publisher.id} ->
${publisher.name}"
            } catch (Exception e) {
```

```
                    return "Unable to add new publisher named ${name}\
n${e.getMessage()}"
            }
        } else {
            return "PublisherRepository is not found!"
        }
    }


    @Usage("Remove existing publisher")
    @Command
    def remove(@Usage("publisher id") @Option(names=["i","id"])
String id, InvocationContext context) {
        PublisherRepository repository =
                            getPublisherRepository(context)
        if (repository) {
            try {
                repository.delete(Long.parseLong(id))
                return "Removed publisher ${id}"
            } catch (Exception e) {
                return "Unable to remove publisher with id ${id}\
n${e.getMessage()}"
            }
        } else {
            return "PublisherRepository is not found!"
        }
    }


    def getPublisherRepository(InvocationContext context) {
        BeanFactory bf =
          context.getAttributes().get("spring.beanfactory")
        PublisherRepository repository =
          bf.getBean(PublisherRepository)
        return repository
    }

}
```

9. With the commands built up, now let's start our application by executing `./gradlew clean bootRun` and then connect to it via SSH by executing `ssh -p 2000 user@ localhost` and log in using the generated password hash.

10. When we type `publishers`, we will see the list of all the possible commands, as follows:

```
> publishers
usage: publishers [-h | --help] COMMAND [ARGS]


The most commonly used publishers commands are:
   add              Add new publisher
   remove           Remove existing publisher
   list             Lists all publishers
```

11. Let's add a publisher by typing `publishers add --name "Fictitious Books"` and we should see a message: `Added new publisher 2 -> Fictitious Books.`

12. If we will now type `publishers list`, we will get a list of all the books:

```
id name
---------
1   Packt
2   Fictitious Books
```

13. Removing a publisher is a simple command: `publishers remove --id 2` that should respond with a message: `Removed publisher 2.`

14. Just to confirm that the publisher is really gone, execute `publishers list` and we should see the following:

```
Available Publishers: id -> name
1 -> Packt
```

How it works...

The Spring Boot integration with CRaSH provides you with many commands out of the box. We can invoke the same management end points that were available to us over HTTP and JMX. We can get access to the JVM information, make changes to the logging configuration, and even interact with the JMX server and all the registered MBeans. The list of all the possibilities is really impressive and very rich in functionalities, so I would definitely advise you to read the reference documentation on CRaSH by going to `http://www.crashub.org/1.3/reference.html`.

In Spring Boot, the expectation is that any groovy file placed in the classpath of `/commands/**` or `/crash/commands/**` will be automatically picked up and registered as a CRaSH command. The name of the class translates into the main command name. In our case, we called the class `publishers` and it became the top-level command name in the CRaSH console.

Until version 1.3, CRaSH only supported Groovy to write the commands but later versions gained the support to do it in pure Java as well; so though Groovy is more convenient for writing these type of scripts, one can do it in plain Java as well. The following are the annotations that we've used in our command definition:

- The @Usage annotation can be used to annotate the class and command methods and parameters to provide a description of the intended usage for the given component. It is a good idea to provide as much description and documentation as possible as in the shell, one would like to clearly educate the users of what needs to happen and how to call the command. The Man pages are great so keep the documentation top notch.

- The @Command annotation indicates that a given method represents a command that is to be executed. If a class has only one method, it is conventional to name it main and it will become the only command for a given class that would be executed when the class name is typed. If we want multiple subcommands to reside in the class command, as we did with publishers, the name of the method will translate into the name of the command.

- The @Option annotation goes in the method argument and provides the short and long option names that would be translated into the argument value, which has to be of the String, Integer, Boolean, or a few other basic types.

- The @Argument annotation also goes in the method argument and indicates that an annotated method argument should be populated from the command-line argument entry. If it is required, an @Required annotation can be used as well.

- InvocationContext is a special object that can be defined as a method argument and it can be used to retrieve the various context-bound elements. Spring Boot registers a number of arguments that can be extracted from the context, as follows:

  - spring.boot.version: This provides a version of Spring Boot.
  - spring.version: This provides a version of Spring.
  - spring.beanfactory: This provides a reference to the Bean Factory instance, which can be used to get access to any of the beans registered in it. We used this to get a reference to the PublisherRepository in our example.
  - spring.environment: This provides a reference to the Spring Environment instance, which can be used to get access to any of the environment properties and configurations.

Each command can be queried for its usage by using --help, just like in most Linux-based command-line tools. Similarly, CRaSH has a notion of man-pages, so typing man <command> will display the detailed instructions, which can be defined by using the @Man annotation so that it can be used in conjunction with @Usage.

While CRaSH comes with many built-in commands, Spring Boot, via remote-shell-starter, adds a few more Spring Boot-specific ones, which are as follows:

- ▶ The `autoconfig` command displays the AutoConfiguration report, which we have seen earlier, showing which conditions have matched and which ones did not.

- ▶ The `beans` command shows all the Spring Beans that exist in the `ApplicationContext`.

- ▶ The `endpoint` command provides a list of all the available endpoints as well as an ability to invoke any of them and get their results. We have seen this in action when we invoked the `healthEndpoint`.

- ▶ The `metrics` command simply prints out all the metrics information on a screen in a nice table layout.

Looking at the code, one might have noticed the different handling of results between the `list` and `add/remove` commands. This is because for the list command we wanted to support the Pipe functionality, which is a very powerful facility that provides you with the ability to stack commands in CRaSH, piping results of one command, as an input to the other, just like in Linux process pipe functionality.

We can chain different commands together so as to help process the output and filter out the necessary data when the amount of information tends to get overwhelming. Imagine that our publishers list command returns not two, but two thousand publishers. From this list, we want to find the ones that start with `Pa`. Using the Pipe functionality, we can easily chain the `publishers list` command with the `filter` command in the following way:

publishers list | filter -p name:Pa*

In our example, this should return us only one record, as follows:

```
id name
---------
1  Packt
```

While not every command—for one reason or other—supports piping, we can easily find out if it does by running the `man` command. For example, if we run `man publishers list`, we will get all the information about the list command:

NAME

        publishers list - Lists all publishers

SYNOPSIS

        publishers [-h | --help] list

STREAM

```
publishers list <java.lang.Void, java.util.Map>
```

PARAMETERS

```
[-h | --help]
    Display this help message
```

The STREAM section gives us the necessary information about what the expected pipe inputs and outputs are. In this case, Void is the expected input, meaning that this command does not accept anything to be piped into it but it does return Map as an output, which can be piped into another command such as filter as an input for processing.

Running man filter will tell us that the filter command accepts Map as a pipe input and will return filtered Map as an output containing the entries that match the provided pattern.

While adding the CRaSH dependencies, we added a compile("org.crashub:crash. connectors.telnet:1.3.1") dependency, which enabled us to connect not only via SSH, but also using the Telnet protocol. The Telnet connection can be established by invoking the telnet localhost 5000 command.

The CRaSH Spring Boot integration comes with a number of configuration options allowing us to disable certain commands or connection methods, configure the authentication settings, and specify usernames, passwords, and even key certificates. For example, if we want to use a specific username and password, we can do so by configuring the following properties:

shell.auth.simple.user.name=remote

shell.auth.simple.user.password=shell

In a real-world enterprise environment, it is more common to use the shared keys for restricted access and these can be configured using the shell.ssh.key-path=<key path> property.

Integrating Codahale/Dropwizard metrics with Graphite

Earlier in this chapter, we learned about the monitoring capabilities that are provided by Spring Boot. We saw examples of writing custom HealthIndicators implementations, creating Metrics, and using GaugeService and CounterService to emit data. The simple Spring Boot Admin Web framework gave us some nice graphical UI to visualize the data, but all of these metrics were in-the-moment, with no long-term retention and historical access. Not being able to observe the trends, detect the deviations from the baseline, and compare today with last week is not a very good strategy, especially for an enterprise complex system. We all want to be able to have access to the time series data going weeks, if not months, back and set up alarms and thresholds, if something goes unplanned.

This recipe will introduce us to an amazing time series graphical tool: Graphite. Graphite is a two-part system. It provides storage for numeric time series data as well as a service to render this data in a form of on-demand graphs or expose the graph data as a JSON stream. We will learn how to utilize another great framework: Codahale/Dropwizard Metrics, in order to send the monitoring data from a Spring Boot application to Graphite and play a bit with Graphite to visualize the different statistics that we've gathered.

Getting ready

Graphite is an application that is written in Python and is thus capable of running on virtually any system supporting Python and its libraries. There are multiple ways of installing Graphite on any given system, ranging from compilation from a source, using `pip` all the way, or to prebuilt RPMs for various Linux distributions.

 For all the different installation strategies, take a look at the Graphite documentation by visiting `http://graphite.readthedocs.org/en/latest/install.html`. OS X users should read a very good step-by-step guide located at `https://gist.github.com/relaxdiego/7539911`.

For the purposes of this recipe, we will use a premade Docker container containing Graphite as well as its counterpart Grafana. While there is an abundance of various prebuilt variants of Docker images containing combinations of Graphite and Grafana, we will use the one from `https://registry.hub.docker.com/u/alexmercer/graphite-grafana/` as it contains all the right configurations that will make it easy for us to get started quickly.

1. The first step will be to download the desired Docker container image. We will do this by executing `docker pull alexmercer/graphite-grafana`. The container size is about 500 MB; so the download might take a few minutes, depending on your connection speed.

2. Both Graphite and Grafana store their data in the database files. We will need to create external directories, which will reside outside the container, and we will connect them to a running instance via Docker Data Volumes in a following way:

    ❑   Make a directory for the Graphite data anywhere in your system, for example, in `<user_home>/data/graphite`

    ❑   Make a directory for the Grafana data, for example, in `<user_home>/data/grafana`

3. In this container, the Graphite data will go to `/var/lib/graphite/storage/whisper`, while Grafana stores its data in `/usr/share/grafana/data`. So, we will use these paths as internal volume mount destinations when starting the container.

4. Run the container by executing `docker run -v <user_home>/data/graphite:/var/lib/graphite/storage/whisper -v <user_home>/data/grafana:/usr/share/grafana/data -p 2003:2003 -p 3000:3000 -p 8888:80 -d alexmercer/graphite-grafana`.

   ❑ In Docker, the `-v` option configures a volume mount binding. In our example, we configured the external `<user_home>/data/graphite` directory to be the same as the `/var/lib/graphite/storage/whisper` directory reference in the container. The same goes for the `<user_home>/data/grafana` mapping. We can even look in the `<user_home>/data/graphite` or `data/grafana` directories to see them contain the subdirectories and files.

   ❑ The `-p` option configures the port mappings similar to the directory volumes. In our example, we mapped three different ports to be accessible from outside the container to the internal ports to which the various services are bound.

   The 2003:2003 port mapping externalizes the Graphite data stream listener known as Carbon-Cache Line Receiver, to which we will connect in order to send the metrics data.

   The 3000:3000 port mapping externalizes the Grafana Web Dashboard UI, which we will use to create visual dashboards on top of the Graphite data.

   The 8888:80 port mapping externalizes the Graphite Web UI. Though it is running on port 80 in the container, it is unlikely that on our development machine, port 80 is open; so it is better to map it to some other higher number port such as 8080 or 8888 in our case, as 8080 is already taken by our `BookPub` application.

5. If everything has gone according to plan, Graphite and Grafana should be up and running and thus, we can access Graphite by pointing our browser to `http://localhost:8888` and we should see the following screen:

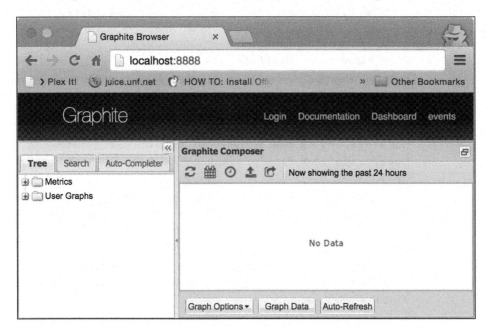

6. To see Grafana, point the browser to `http://localhost:3000` so as to see the following screen:

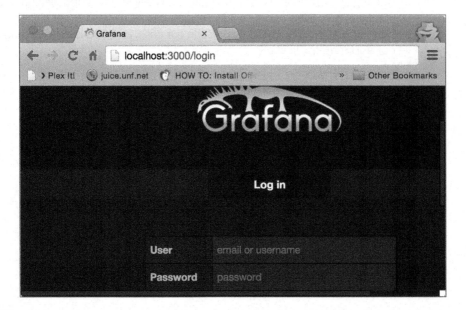

7. The default login and password for Grafana are `admin/admin` and can be changed via the web UI admin.

> For the OS X users who use `boot2docker`, the IP would not be of the localhost, but rather a result of the boot2docker ip call.

8. Once we are in Grafana, we will need to add our Graphite instance as a Data Source entry, so click on the 🔘 icon, go to **Data Sources**, and add a new source of Type: `Graphite`, Url: `http://localhost:80`, Access: `proxy`.

How to do it...

With Graphite and Grafana up and running, we are now ready to start configuring our application in order to send the metrics to the Graphite listener on port 2003. To do this, we will use the Codahale/Dropwizard Metrics library, which is fully supported by Spring Boot and thus requires a minimum amount of configuration.

1. The first thing on our list is to add the necessary library dependencies. Extend the dependencies block in `build.gradle` with the following content:

```
compile("io.dropwizard.metrics:metrics-core:3.1.0")
compile("io.dropwizard.metrics:metrics-jvm:3.1.0")
compile("io.dropwizard.metrics:metrics-graphite:3.1.0")
```

2. We will also add the following dependency to `build.gradle` located in the `db-count-starter` directory at the root of our project:

```
compile("io.dropwizard.metrics:metrics-core:3.1.0")
```

3. Create a file named `MonitoringConfiguration.java` in the `src/main/java/org/test/bookpub` directory at the root of our project with the following content:

```
@Configuration
class MonitoringConfiguration {

    @Bean
    public Graphite graphite(@Value("${graphite.host}")
                                     String graphiteHost,
                              @Value("${graphite.port}")
                                     int graphitePort) {
        return new Graphite(
          new InetSocketAddress(graphiteHost, graphitePort));
    }

    @Bean
```

```
        public GraphiteReporter graphiteReporter(Graphite graphite,
                                                  MetricRegistry
    registry) {
            GraphiteReporter reporter =
                    GraphiteReporter.forRegistry(registry)
                    .prefixedWith("bookpub.app")
                    .convertRatesTo(TimeUnit.SECONDS)
                    .convertDurationsTo(TimeUnit.MILLISECONDS)
                    .filter(MetricFilter.ALL)
                    .build(graphite);
            reporter.start(1, TimeUnit.MINUTES);

            return reporter;
        }


        @Bean
        public MemoryUsageGaugeSet memoryUsageGaugeSet(MetricRegistry
    registry) {
            MemoryUsageGaugeSet memoryUsageGaugeSet =
                            new MemoryUsageGaugeSet();
            registry.register("memory", memoryUsageGaugeSet);
            return memoryUsageGaugeSet;
        }
        @Bean
        public ThreadStatesGaugeSet
          threadStatesGaugeSet(MetricRegistry registry) {
            ThreadStatesGaugeSet threadStatesGaugeSet =
                            new ThreadStatesGaugeSet();
            registry.register("threads", threadStatesGaugeSet);
            return threadStatesGaugeSet;
        }
    }
```

4. We will also need to add the configuration property settings for our Graphite instance to the `application.properties` file in the `src/main/resources` directory at the root of our project:

```
graphite.host=localhost
graphite.port=2003
```

5. To complete the changes, we will make small changes to the `DbCountMetrics`. `java` file in `db-count-starter/src/main/java/org/test/bookpubstarter/dbcount` with the following content:

```java
public class DbCountMetrics implements PublicMetrics, MetricSet {

    ...

    @Override
    public Map<String, com.codahale.metrics.Metric> getMetrics() {
        final Map<String, com.codahale.metrics.Metric> gauges =
                new HashMap<String, com.codahale.metrics.Metric>();
        for (Metric springMetric : metrics()) {
            gauges.put(springMetric.getName(),
                        (Gauge<Number>) springMetric::getValue);
        }
        return gauges;
    }
}
```

6. We will make another small change to the `dbCountMetrics` method in the `DbCountAutoConfiguration.java` file, also in `db-count-starter/src/main/java/org/test/bookpubstarter/dbcount`, with the following changes:

```java
@Configuration
public class DbCountAutoConfiguration {

    ...

    @Bean
    public PublicMetrics dbCountMetrics(
                            Collection<CrudRepository>
                                repositories,
                            MetricRegistry registry) {
        DbCountMetrics dbCountMetrics = new
            DbCountMetrics(repositories);
        registry.registerAll(dbCountMetrics);
        return dbCountMetrics;
    }
}
```

7. Now, let's build and run our application by executing `./gradlew clean bootRun` and if we have configured everything correctly, it should start without any issues.

8. With the application up and running, we should start seeing some data appearing in the Graphite and, and, and we will see `bookpub` data nodes getting added to the tree under `Metrics`. To add some more realism, let's open our browser and load a book URL, `http://localhost:8080/books/978-1-78528-415-1/`, a few dozen times to generate some metrics.

9. Let's go ahead and look at some of the metrics in Graphite and set the data time range to 15 minutes in order to get some close-look graphs, which is as follows:

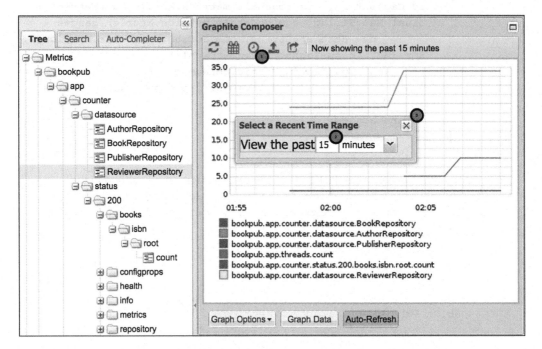

10. We can also create some fancy looking dashboards using this data in Grafana by creating a new Dashboard and adding a **Graph** panel, as shown in the following screenshot:

11. The newly created **Graph** panel will appear as follows:

12. Click on the **no title (click here)** label, choose **edit,** and enter the metric name
    `bookpub.app.counter.status.200.books.isbn.root.count` in the
    text field:

13. Clicking **Back to dashboard** will take you out of the edit mode.

 For a more detailed tutorial, see `http://docs.grafana.org/`
`guides/gettingstarted/`.

How it works...

To add the Dropwizard metrics, we will add the following three new dependencies to our
build file:

- `core`: This adds the basic Dropwizard functionality, the `MetricsRegistry`,
  common API interfaces, and base classes. This is the bare minimum that is required
  to get Dropwizard working and integrated into Spring Boot to handle the metrics.

- `jvm`: This adds a number of `GaugeSets` that expose the various JVM-related metrics
  and can be registered with `MetricsRegistry`. We used `MemoryUsageGuageSet`
  and `ThreadStatesGaugeSet` to demonstrate how the JVM runtime data can
  be sent to Graphite. These metrics expose the Heap and Non-Heap memory pool
  statistics and the Thread information, such as how many threads are created, which
  ones are active, waiting, blocked, and so on.

- `graphite`: This adds support for `GraphiteReporter` and is needed in
  order to configure Dropwizard to send the monitoring data that it collects
  to our Graphite instance.

In order to keep things clean and nicely separated, we created a separate configuration class with all the monitoring-related beans and settings: `MonitoringConfiguration`. In this class, we configured four `@Bean` instances: first was the Graphite instance, which has a dependency on two configuration values, defined in `application.properties`, specifying the host/ip and port of our Graphite instance.

Second was the `GraphiteReporter`, which is dependent on `Graphite` and `MetricsRegistry`, and configured so as to send the data to the `Graphite` instance every one minute, use `bookpub.app` as a base tree node hierarchy, and translate all the time duration intervals, such as the latency measurements, into milliseconds and all the variable rates, such as the number of requests per some time frame, into seconds. These values are the default configuration settings for Graphite but can be changed, if desired.

The other two beans are the `MemoryUsageGuageSet` and `ThreadStatesGaugeSet` instances, which are registered with `MetricsRegistry`, and expose the memory and thread metrics to `Graphite` in the memory and threads data nodes. They can be found in `Metrics/bookpub/app/memory` or `Metrics/bookpub/app/threads` nodes in the Graphite tree.

You have probably noticed that we added the `metrics-core` dependency to our `db-count-starter` subproject as well. This was done so that we can expose our `DbCountMetrics` data not only via the HTTP `/metrics` endpoint, but see it in Graphite as well. The reason for this change is the fact that the `PublicMetrics` implementations are being exposed only via the `/metrics` endpoint and they don't get registered with the `GaugeService` or `CoutnerService` providers. Luckily for us, the Dropwizard Metrics provide a very rich API in the form of `MetricSet`, which allows us to wrap anything and expose it as an encapsulated set of metrics, register this wrapper with the `MetricRegistry` and this will automatically expose the data to all the configured reporters. The `MemoryUsageGuageSet` and `ThreadStatesGaugeSet` implementations are a good example. They wrap the various JVM system data and provide it as a set of metrics to the `MetricRegistry`.

Having implemented `MetricSet`, `DbCountMetrics` now implements the `getMetrics()` method, which just translates the result of the existing `metrics()` call, returns a map of simple values that are implemented as the Java 8 Lambda expressions for the `Gauge` interface, thus returning a result of the `springMetric::getValue` method call.

With this small enhancement, we will add `MetricRegistry` as an argument to the `dbCountMetrics(...)` bean creating method in the `DbCountAutoConfiguration` class that in addition to creating the `DbCountMetrics` instance, registers it with `MetricRegistry` before returning it.

The running application will gather all the metrics registered with `MetricRegistry` and every configured reporter—in our case: `GraphiteReporter`—reports all these metrics at a timed interval to its destination. The proper `Reporter` implementations run in a separate `ThreadPool`, thus outside of the main application threads and not interfering with them. However, this should be kept in mind in case the `Metric` implementations use some `ThreadLocal` data internally, which would not be available to Reporters.

Integrating Codahale/Dropwizard metrics with Dashing

The previous recipe has given us a glimpse of how we can collect the various metrics from our application during its runtime We've also seen how powerful the ability to visualize this data as a set of graphs of historical trends can be.

While Grafana and Graphite offers us a very powerful capability of manipulating the data in the form of graphs and building elaborate dashboards that are full of thresholds, applied data functions, and much more. Sometimes we want something simpler, more readable, and something widgetty. This is exactly the kind of dashboard experience that is provided by Dashing.

Dashing is a popular dashboard framework developed by Shopify and written in Ruby/Sinatra. It provides you with an ability to create an assortment of dashboards that are comprised of different types of widgets. We can have things such as Graphs, Meters, Lists, Numeric values, or just plain Text to display the information.

In this recipe, we will install the Dashing framework, learn how to create dashboards, send and consume the data to report from an application directly as well as fetching it from Graphite, and using Dashing API to push the data to the Dashing instance.

Getting ready

In order to get Dashing to run, we will need to have an environment that has a Ruby 1.9+ installed with Ruby Gems.

 Typically, Ruby should be available on any common distribution of Linux and OS X. If you are running Windows, I would suggest using `http://rubyinstaller.org` in order to get the installation bundle.

Once you have such an environment available, we will install Dashing and create a new dashboard application for our use, as follows:

1. Installing Dashing is very easy; simply execute the `gem install dashing` command to install Dashing Ruby Gem in your system.

2. With the gem successfully installed, we will create the new dashboard named `bookpub_dashboard` by executing the `dashing new bookpub_dashboard` command in the directory where you want the dashboard application to be created.

3. Once the dashboard application has been generated, go to the `bookpub_dashboard` directory and execute the `bundle` command to install the needed dependency gems.

4. After the gems bundle has been installed, we can start the dashboard application by executing the `dashing start` command and then pointing our browser to `http://localhost:3030` to see the following result:

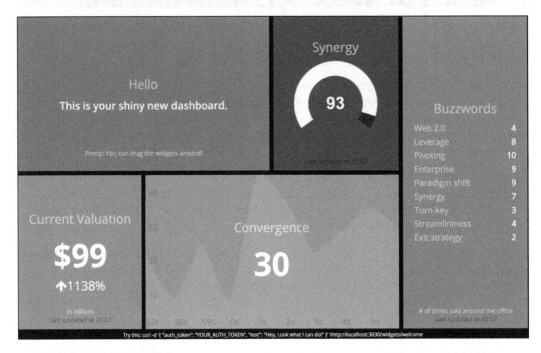

How to do it...

If you look carefully at the URL of our shiny new dashboard, you will see that it actually says `http://localhost:3030/sample` and displays a sample dashboard that was automatically generated. We will use this sample dashboard to make some changes in order to display some metrics from our application directly as well as get some raw metrics from the Graphite data API endpoint.

To demonstrate how to connect the data from the application `/metrics` endpoint so as to display it in the Dashing dashboard, we will change the Buzzwords widget to display the counts of our data repositories, as follows:

1. Before we start, we will need to add the `gem 'httparty', '>= 0.13.3'` gem to `Gemfile` located in the `bookpub_dashboard` directory, which will enable us to use an HTTP client in order to extract the monitoring metrics from the HTTP endpoints.

2. After adding the gem, run the `bundle` command one more time to install the newly added gem.

3. Next, we will need to modify the `sample.erb` dashboard definition located in the `bookpub_dashboard/dashboards` directory, replacing `<div data-id="buzzwords" data-view="List" data-unordered="true" data-title="Buzzwords" data-moreinfo="# of times said around the office"></div>` with `<div data-id="repositories" data-view="List" data-unordered="true" data-title="Repositories Count" data-moreinfo="# of entries in data repositories"></div>`.

4. With the widget replaced, we will create a new data provisioning job file named `repo_counters.rb` in the `bookpub_dashboard/jobs` directory with the following content:

```
require 'httparty'

repos = ['AuthorRepository', 'ReviewerRepository',
'BookRepository', 'PublisherRepository']

SCHEDULER.every '10s' do
  data = JSON.parse(HTTParty.get("http://localhost:8080/metrics").
body)
  repo_counts = []

  repos.each do |repo|
    current_count = data["counter.datasource.#{repo}"]
    repo_counts << { label: repo, value: current_count }
  end

  send_event('repositories', { items: repo_counts })
end
```

5. With all the code changes in place, let's start our dashboard by executing the `dashing start` command. Go to `http://localhost:3030/sample` in the browser to see our new widget displaying the data as shown in the following image:

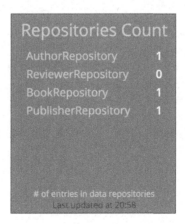

6. If we use the remote shell to log in to the application, as we did earlier in this chapter, and add a publisher, we would see the counter on the dashboard increase.

7. Another way to push the data to the dashboard is to use their RESTful API. Let's update the text in the top left text widget by executing `curl -d '{ "auth_token": "YOUR_AUTH_TOKEN", "text": "My RESTful dashboard update!" }' http://localhost:3030/widgets/welcome`.

8. If everything has worked correctly, we should see the text updated to our new value, `My RESTful dashboard update!`, under the `Hello` title.

9. In an environment where multiple instances of the same application kind are running, it is probably not a good idea to directly pull the data from each node, especially if they are very dynamic and can come and go as they please. It is advised that you consume the data from a more static and well-known location, such as a Graphite instance. To get a demonstration of volatile data metrics, we will consume the memory pool data for the **Eden**, **Survivor**, and **OldGen** spaces and display them instead of the `Convergence`, `Synergy`, and `Valuation` graph dashboards. We will start by replacing the content of the `sample.rb` job file located in the `bookpub_dashboard/jobs` directory with the following content:

```ruby
require 'httparty'
require 'date'

eden_key = "bookpub.app.memory.pools.PS-Eden-Space.usage"
survivor_key = "bookpub.app.memory.pools.PS-Survivor-Space.usage"
oldgen_key = "bookpub.app.memory.pools.PS-Old-Gen.usage"

SCHEDULER.every '60s' do

data = JSON.parse(HTTParty.get("http://localhost:8888/
render/?from=-11minutes&target=bookpub.app.memory.pools.PS-Eden-
Space.usage&target=bookpub.app.memory.pools.PS-Survivor-Space.
usage&target=bookpub.app.memory.pools.PS-Old-Gen.usage&format=json
&maxDataPoints=11").body)

  data.each do |metric|
    target = metric["target"]
    # Remove the last data point, which typically has empty value
    data_points = metric["datapoints"][0...-1]
    if target == eden_key
      points = []
      data_points.each_with_index do |entry, idx|
        value = 100 * entry[0] rescue 0
```

```
          points << { x: entry[1], y: value.round(0)}
        end
        send_event('heap_eden', points: points)
      elsif target == survivor_key
        current_survivor = 100 * data_points.last[0] rescue 0
        send_event("heap_survivor", { value: current_survivor.
round(2)})
      elsif target == oldgen_key
        current_oldgen = 100 * data_points.last[0] rescue 0
        last_oldgen = 100 * data_points[-2][0] rescue 0
        send_event("heap_oldgen", { current: current_oldgen.
round(2), last: last_oldgen.round(2)})
      end
    end
end
```

10. In the `sample.erb` template located in the `bookpub_dashboard/dashboards` directory, we will replace the `synergy`, `valuation`, and `convergence` graphs with the following alternatives:

    □ `<div data-id="synergy" data-view="Meter" data-title="Synergy" data-min="0" data-max="100"></div>` gets replaced with `<div data-id="heap_survivor" data-view="Meter" data-title="Heap: Survivor" data-min="0" data-max="100"></div>`

    □ `<div data-id="valuation" data-view="Number" data-title="Current Valuation" data-moreinfo="In billions" data-prefix="$"></div>` gets replaced with `<div data-id="heap_oldgen" data-view="Number" data-title="Heap: OldGen" data-moreinfo="In %" data-suffix="%"></div>`

    □ `<div data-id="convergence" data-view="Graph" data-title="Convergence" style="background-color:#ff9618"></div>` gets replaced with `<div data-id="heap_eden" data-view="Graph" data-title="Heap: Eden" style="background-color:#ff9618"></div>`

11. After all the changes are made, we can restart the dashboard application and reload our browser to `http://localhost:3030` to see the following result:

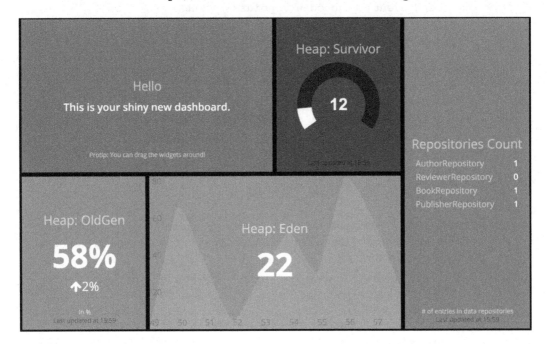

How it works...

In this recipe, we have seen how to extract the data directly from our application and via Graphite and render it using the Dashing dashboard as well as pushing information directly to Dashing using their RESTful API. It is no secret that it is better to see something once than hear about it seven times. This is true when it comes to trying to get a holistic picture of the key metrics that represent how the systems behave at runtime and to be able to act on the data quickly.

Without going in great detail about the internals of Dashing, it is still important to mention a few things about how data gets in Dashing. This can happen in the following two ways:

▶ **Scheduled Jobs**: This is used to pull data from the external sources
▶ **RESTful API**: This is used to push data to Dashing from outside

The scheduled jobs are defined in the `jobs` directory in the generated dashboard application. Each file has a piece of ruby code wrapped in the `SCHEDULER.every` block, which computes the data points and sends an event to an appropriate widget with the new data for an update.

In our recipe, we created a new job named `repo_counters.rb` where we used the `httparty` library in order to make a direct call to our application instance's `/metrics` endpoint and extracted the counters for each of the predefined repositories. Looping over the metrics, we created a `repo_counts` collection with data for each repository containing a label display and a value count. The resulting collection was sent to the repositories widget for an update in the form of an event: `send_event('repositories', { items: repo_counts })`.

We configured this job to get executed every ten seconds, but if the rate of data change is not very frequent, the number can be changed to a few minutes or even hours. Every time the scheduler runs our job, the `repositories` widget gets updated via the client-side websockets communication with the new data. Looking in `dashboards/sample.erb`, we can find the widget's definition using `data-id="repositories"`.

Besides adding our own new job, we also changed the existing `sample.rb` job to pull data from Graphite using Graphite's RESTful API to populate the different types of widgets in order to display the memory heap data. As we were not pulling data directly from the application instance, it was a good idea not to put the code in the same job because the jobs could—and in our case, do—have different time intervals. As we send data to Graphite only once every minute, it does not make sense to pull it any less frequently than this.

To get the data out of Graphite, we used the following API call:

```
/render/?from=-11minutes&target=bookpub.app.memory.pools.PS-Eden-
Space.usage&target=bookpub.app.memory.pools.PS-Survivor-Space.
usage&target=bookpub.app.memory.pools.PS-Old-Gen.usage&format=json&maxDat
aPoints=11
```

It translates into the following components:

- ▶ `target`: This parameter is a repeated value that defines a list of all the different metrics that we want to retrieve.

- ▶ `from`: This parameter specifies the time range; in our case, we asked for data going back to 11 minutes back.

- ▶ `format`: This parameter configures the desired output format. We chose JSON but many others are available. Refer to `http://graphite.readthedocs.org/en/latest/render_api.html#format`.

- ▶ `maxDataPoints`: This parameter indicates how many entries we want to get.

The reason we asked for eleven entries and not ten is due to a frequent occurrence where the last entry of short-ranged requests, which consist of only a few minutes, sometimes get returned as empty. We just use the first ten entries and ignore the most recent ones to avoid weird data visualization.

Iterating over the target data, we will populate the appropriate `widgets`, `heap_eden`, `heap_survivor`, and `heap_oldgen`, with their designated data, as follows:

▶ `heap_eden`: This is a `Graph` widget, as defined in the `sample.erb` template in the form of a `data-view="Graph"` attribute, so it wants a data input in the form of the `points` collection containing a value for *x* and *y*. The *x* value represents a timestamp, which conveniently gets returned to us by Graphite and is automatically converted to the minutes display value by the `Graph` widget. The *y* value represents the memory pool utilization in percent. As the value from Graphite is in the form of a decimal number, we will need to convert it to a whole number so as to make it look better.

▶ `heap_survivor`: This is a `Meter` widget, as defined in the `sample.erb` template in the form of a `data-view="Meter"` attribute, so it wants a data input as a simple value number between a template configured range. In our case, the range is set as the `data-min="0"` `data-max="100"` attributes. Even though we chose to round the number to two decimal positions, it could probably just be an integer as it is precise enough for the purpose of a dashboard display.

▶ `heap_oldgen`: This is a `Number` widget, as defined in the `sample.erb` template in the form of a `data-view="Number"` attribute, so it wants a data input as a current value and optionally a last value; in which case, a percentage change with the change direction will be displayed as well. As we get the last ten entries, we have no issues in retrieving both the current and last values so we can easily satisfy this requirement.

In this recipe, we also experimented with Dashing's RESTful API by trying to use a `curl` command to update the value of the welcome widget. This was a push operation and can be used in situations where there is no data API exposed, but you have a capability of creating some sort of a script or piece of code that could send the data to Dashing instead. To achieve this, we used the following command: `curl -d '{ "auth_token": "YOUR_AUTH_TOKEN", "text": "My RESTful dashboard update!" }' http://localhost:3030/widgets/welcome`.

The Dashing API accepts data in a JSON format, sent via a POST request that contains the parameters needed for the widgets as well as the widget ID which is a part of the URL path itself. The following are the accepted URL parameters:

▶ `auth_token`: This allows for a secure data update and can be configured in the dashboard root directory in the `config.ru` file.

▶ `text`: This is a widget property that is being changed. As we are updating a `Text` widget, as defined in the `sample.erb` template in the form of a `data-view="Text"` attribute, we need to send it the `text` attribute for an update.

▶ `/widgets/<widget id>`: This URL path identifies the particular widget where the update is destined to. This id corresponds to a declaration in the `sample.erb` template. In our case, it looks like `data-id="welcome"`.

The definition of the various widgets can also be manipulated and a very rich collection of the various widgets has been created by the community, which is available at `https://github.com/Shopify/dashing/wiki/Additional-Widgets`. The widgets get installed in the `widgets` directory in the dashboard and can be installed by simply running `dashing install GIST` where GIST is the hash of the GitHub Gist entry.

The dashboard template files, similar to our `sample.erb`, can be modified in order to create the desired layout for each particular dashboard as well as multiple dashboard templates, which can be rotated or directly loaded manually.

Each dashboard represents a grid in which the various widgets get placed. Each widget is defined by a `<div>` entry with the appropriate configuration attributes and it should be nested in the `<li>` grid element. We can use the following data element attributes to control the positioning of each widget in the grid:

- `data-row`: This represents the row number where the widget should be positioned
- `data-col`: This represents the column number where the widget should be positioned
- `data-sizex`: This defines the number of columns the widget will span horizontally
- `data-sizey`: This defines the number of rows the widget will span vertically

The existing widgets can be modified to change their look and feel as well as extend their functionality; so the sky is the limit for what kind of information display we can have. You should definitely check out `http://dashing.io` for more details.

Index

U

W

Thank you for buying
Spring Boot Cookbook

About Packt Publishing

Packt, pronounced 'packed', published its first book, *Mastering phpMyAdmin for Effective MySQL Management*, in April 2004, and subsequently continued to specialize in publishing highly focused books on specific technologies and solutions.

Our books and publications share the experiences of your fellow IT professionals in adapting and customizing today's systems, applications, and frameworks. Our solution-based books give you the knowledge and power to customize the software and technologies you're using to get the job done. Packt books are more specific and less general than the IT books you have seen in the past. Our unique business model allows us to bring you more focused information, giving you more of what you need to know, and less of what you don't.

Packt is a modern yet unique publishing company that focuses on producing quality, cutting-edge books for communities of developers, administrators, and newbies alike. For more information, please visit our website at www.packtpub.com.

About Packt Open Source

In 2010, Packt launched two new brands, Packt Open Source and Packt Enterprise, in order to continue its focus on specialization. This book is part of the Packt open source brand, home to books published on software built around open source licenses, and offering information to anybody from advanced developers to budding web designers. The Open Source brand also runs Packt's open source Royalty Scheme, by which Packt gives a royalty to each open source project about whose software a book is sold.

Writing for Packt

We welcome all inquiries from people who are interested in authoring. Book proposals should be sent to author@packtpub.com. If your book idea is still at an early stage and you would like to discuss it first before writing a formal book proposal, then please contact us; one of our commissioning editors will get in touch with you.

We're not just looking for published authors; if you have strong technical skills but no writing experience, our experienced editors can help you develop a writing career, or simply get some additional reward for your expertise.

Mastering Spring Application Development

ISBN: 978-1-78398-732-0   Paperback: 288 pages

Gain expertise in developing and caching your applications running on the JVM with Spring

1. Build full-featured web applications, such as Spring MVC applications, efficiently that will get you up and running with Spring web development.

2. Reuse working code snippets handy for integration scenarios such as Twitter, e-mail, FTP, databases, and many others.

3. An advanced guide which includes Java programs to integrate Spring with Thymeleaf.

Spring MVC Beginner's Guide

ISBN: 978-1-78328-487-0   Paperback: 304 pages

Your ultimate guide to building a complete web application using all the capabilities of Spring MVC

1. Carefully crafted exercises, with detailed explanations for each step, to help you understand the concepts with ease.

2. You will gain a clear understanding of the end to end request/response life cycle, and each logical component's responsibility.

3. Packed with tips and tricks that will demonstrate the industry best practices on developing a Spring-MVC-based application.

Please check **www.PacktPub.com** for information on our titles

Spring Security 3.x Cookbook

ISBN: 978-1-78216-752-5   Paperback: 300 pages

Over 60 recipes to help you successfully safeguard your web applications with Spring Security

1. Learn about all the mandatory security measures for modern day applications using Spring Security.

2. Investigate different approaches to application level authentication and authorization.

3. Master how to mount security on applications used by developers and organizations.

Spring Security [Video]

ISBN: 978-1-78216-865-2   Duration: 02:10 hours

An empirical approach to securing your web applications

1. Fully secure your web application with Spring Security.

2. Implement authentication and registration with the database as well as with LDAP.

3. Utilize authorization examples that help guide you through the authentication of users step-by-step.

4. Learn with precise and practical examples for advanced security scenarios such as ACL, REST, and Remember Me.

Please check **www.PacktPub.com** for information on our titles

CPSIA information can be obtained
at www.ICGtesting.com
Printed in the USA
LVOW04s1555020617
536736LV00004B/339/P